Perspectives
The Multidisciplinary Series of Physical Education and Sport Science

Volume 3

THE BUSINESS OF SPORT

ICSSPE

CIEPSS

International Council of Sport Science and Physical Education (ICSSPE)

Perspectives
The Multidisciplinary Series of Physical Education and Sport Science

Volume 3

THE BUSINESS OF SPORT

Darlene Kluka & Guido Schilling, Editors

Meyer & Meyer Sport

British Library Cataloguing in Publication Data
A catalogue record for this book is available from the British Library

The Business of Sport/
Darlene Kluka & Guido Schilling (eds.).
– Oxford : Meyer & Meyer Sport (UK) Ltd., 2001
(Perspectives – The Interdisciplinary Series of
Physical Education and Sport Science ; Vol.3)
ISBN 1-84126-056-8

© 2001 by Meyer & Meyer Sport (UK) Ltd
Oxford, Aachen, Olten (CH), Vienna, Québec,
Lansing/Michigan, Adelaide, Auckland, Johannesburg, Budapest
Member of the World
Sportpublishers' Association
www.w-s-p-a.org

Editor: Steve Bailey
Managing Editor: Deena Scoretz
Layout and Typesetting: Deena Scoretz
Cover Design: axept, Berlin
Printed and bound in Germany by
Druckpunkt Offset GmbH, Bergheim
e-mail: verlag@meyer-meyer-sports.com
www.meyer-meyer-sports.com
ISBN 1-84126-056-8

Perspectives - The Multidisciplinary Series of
Physical Education and Sport Science
Volume 3, March 2001

THE BUSINESS OF SPORT

Contents

THE BUSINESS OF SPORT

Contributing Authors

Darlene Kluka (Editor)

Dr. Kluka is an established scholar at the national and international levels in the areas of sports vision research and sport leadership. Since earning a PhD in motor learning from Texas Woman's University, she has been the recipient of the first International Council for Health, Physical Education, Recreation, Sport, and Dance (ICHPERSD) Biennial Scholar in Sport Science Award (1995), the National Association for Girls and Women in Sport Honor Award (1996), the Women's Sports Foundation President's Award (1996), USA Volleyball's Leader in Volleyball Award (1998), the first American Volleyball Coaches Association Excellence in Education Award (1999), Illinois State University Alumnae Association Outstanding Achievements Award (1997), the International Academy of Sports Vision Joe Andera Research Award (1999), SAWPASH Research Award (1994), the Louisiana AHPERD Scholar Award (1999), and the Southern District AAHPERD Scholar Award (2001). She is an AAHPERD Research Fellow (1993) and an Honorary Research Fellow at the Hong Kong Baptist University's Research Center (1998). She was the Founding Co-Editor of the *International Journal of Sports Vision* for 6 years, and is presently serving as the Founding Editor of the *International Journal of Volleyball Research*.

Dr. Kluka is presently Vice President for Research of the International Academy of Sports Vision; Director of ICHPERSD Girls and Women in Sport Commission; a Charter member of the USA Volleyball Sports Medicine and Performance Commission; and is on the Executive Board of the International Council for Sport Science and Physical Education (ICSSPE). She was also appointed to the prestigious ICSSPE Editorial Board (1997). She is the author of several textbooks, including *Volleyball* (4th ed., 2000), and *Motor Behavior: From Learning to Performance* (1999). She has had over 40 internationally and nationally refereed journal articles published in the areas of women in sport, Olympic Movement, and sports vision research. Dr. Kluka has presented numerous professional/research papers world-wide. Her research interests include visual perception and motor behaviour, with a particular regard for volleyball and women in sport. Most recently, the Women's Sports Foundation has named an award in her honour: The Darlene A. Kluka Women's Sports and Activity Research Award (2000).

Guido Schilling (Editor)

Dr. Guido Schilling is a lecturer in psychology and sport psychology at the Swiss Federal Institute of Technology in Zürich. He was a physical education teacher and received his PhD in 1967 from Zürich University in Applied Psychology. He has taught at the Universities of Basel, Bern, Hamburg and the Swiss Sport School in Magglingen. In addition to teaching, he has also been involved in the coaching and counselling of teams and high level athletes. On the FEPSAC (Fédération Européenne de Psychologie des Sports et des Activités Corporelles) he served as president from 1975-1983. He edited over 20 publications on sport science and sport psychology. In 1986, he was elected to the Executive Board of ICSSPE and he served as Chair of ICSSPE's Editorial Board from 1998-2000.

Dion Klein

Dr. Klein has been an educator and businessperson for over 15 years nationally and internationally in the areas of sport management, health and fitness. He has an earned Doctorate in Sports Administration and other post-graduate degrees in Higher Education and Internet Marketing. He is currently studying his MBA at Charles Sturt University (Australia). After teaching at the University of Canberra, he became the Internet Strategist for MIMS Data Systems/Havas MediMedia Australia. He is currently President of Diverse Concepts International and co-founder/CEO of ProfessorMoe.

Don Jones

Don Jones has had a tremendous amount of experience nationally and internationally in the sport and fitness industry. He previously managed the

Participation Division at the Australian Sports Commission with experience in developing policy, strategy, and evaluation frameworks. He is currently the Manager of Industry Training at Sport Industry Australia (Canberra) as well as co-founder/CEO of ProfessorMoe.

William F. Stier, Jr.

Dr. William F. Stier, Jr., a full professor since 1980, directs the undergraduate sport management/graduate athletic administration programs at the State University of New York, Brockport. He has served as President and CEO of several corporations within the sport, recreation and fitness industry and as a paid consultant for numerous organizations including secondary and university sport programs.

Dr. Stier has spoken at 165 conferences and conventions, conducted workshops and sport clinics and served as a management consultant in Singapore, Mexico, Korea, St. Kitts-Nevis, Korea, Republic of China, Canada, Hong Kong, the US, and Malaysia. An author of 253 articles, he has served on the editorial boards of 12 international and national journals and is currently the editor of two journals: *The Physical Educator* and the *International Journal of Sport Management*. He has authored 15 books and a monograph titled: *Alternative Career Paths in Physical Education: Sport Management*.

Recognised as the Researcher of the Year on two occasions (1988 & 1995) within New York State, he received the Merit Award in Physical Education twice (1986 & 1989) in the United States. A Research Fellow (1985), he received the 1st Annual Sport Management Achievement Award in "honor of extensive contributions to the field of Sport Management" in 1999.

Masaru Ikeda – 1940-2000

Prof. Ikeda taught at Osaka University of Health and Sport Sciences where he was a dean of the department for sport for all. Prof. Ikeda was a pioneer of the concept of Sport for All in Japan through tireless efforts in education and publications. His innovative work, *The Sports White Paper*, which happened to be his last work will be published by the Sasakawa Sports Foundation in March 2001. As an educator, Prof. Ikeda brought forth many scholars and researchers in the field of Sport for All and sport management. He held the following positions: Professor, Osaka University of Health and Sport Science, Japan; Vice President, Asiania Sport For All Association (ASFAA); Member of the Board of Directors, Sasakawa Sports Foundation (SSF); Member of the Council on Health and Physical Education, The Ministry of Education, Science Sports and Culture (MESSC); Chairman, The Japanese Society of Sport Sociology.

Prof. Masaru Ikeda passed away on October 27th, 2000 from liver failure at the age of 60. He will be missed as an excellent scholar as well as a beloved educator.

Denver Hendricks

Denver Hendricks completed his Bachelor of Arts and Bachelor of Arts (Honours) degrees in Physical Education at Rhodes University in Grahamstown. In 1981, he was awarded a Fulbright scholarship to study in the USA and completed a Masters Degree at the University of California at Berkley under the mentorship of Harry Edwards, the driving force behind the Olympic Programme for Human Rights and the protests of black American athletes against racial injustices in the USA.

He started his professional career at Dower College in Port Elizabeth in 1980 and proceed from there to Athlone College in Paarl. In 1985, he was appointed lecturer in Physical Education at the University of the Western Cape, specialising in the Sociology of Sport. He was subsequently appointed Senior Lecturer and Professor and Head of the Department of Physical Education at the University. In 1993 he was appointed as Deputy Dean in the Faculty of Arts and served on various University Committees.

After serving as Director (dean) of Students at the University of Port Elizabeth he was appointed as Chief Director in the National Department of Sport (1997). In 1999, he was appointed Acting Director General of National Department of Sport and Recreation and in July 2000 he was appointed Head of Sport and Recreation South Africa. Denver Hendricks serves on various boards and committees of organisations, which have an interest in sport and recreation issues.

Laurence Chalip

Laurence Chalip is an Associate Professor in the School of Marketing and Management at Griffith University, where he convenes the sport management major and serves as co-ordinator of postgraduate studies. Prior to joining Griffith University, he served as director of the graduate program in sport management at the University of Maryland. He currently directs the Olympic Leveraging Project for Australia's Co-operative Research Centre for Sustainable Tourism, and was a principle investigator with the research team evaluating the volunteer program at the Sydney Olympics. He has published over 50 scholarly articles and book chapters, as well as two books. He is editor of the *Sport Management Review* and associate editor of the *Journal of Sport Management*. In 2000, he was awarded the International Chair of Olympism by the Centre d'Etudis Olímpics i de l'Esport at the Universitat Autònoma de Barcelona in co-operation with the IOC.

B. Christine Green

Dr. Green received her PhD in Sport Management at the University of Maryland. She is a Senior Lecturer in the School of Marketing and Management at Griffith University where she convenes the Honours degree and teaches in the sport management program. She served as the Director of Planning and Marketing for Australian University Sport-North, and was a member of the Committee for the National Integration of University Sport. She has published 17 peer reviewed papers, and is a member of the editorial board for four journals in the field of sport management. She led the research team evaluating the volunteer program at the Sydney Olympics, and served as Director of Volunteer Systems for the British Olympic Holding Camp.

Karin J. Buchholz

Karin J. Buchholz is the director of Foreign & Cultural Affairs for the U.S. Olympic Committee. Her responsibilities include being a liaison to North, South, and Central America and the Caribbean, focusing on supporting San Antonio, Texas with their bid effort to capture the 2007 Pan American Games. She oversees the USOC's involvement and participation in the

International Olympic Committee's cultural and art initiatives, the USOC's Office of Protocol & Foreign Activities, and the promotion of women in the Olympic Movement.

Prior to her position with the International Relations Department, Karin Buchholz was the director of Athlete Development for the USOC. The department was created to implement high quality sports programs in communities across the country to help talented and motivated athletes realise their Olympic dreams. She is a frequent USOC representative at events around the world promoting youth sports and athlete development, as well as speaking on women's sport issues and motivation in both English and Spanish.

Before joining the USOC in 1996, Karin Buchholz worked for the U.S. Tennis Association leading a national initiative to increase participation in the sport. Prior to the position at the USTA, she was the executive director and head tennis professional of the Harlem Junior Tennis Program in New York. Under her direction, the program was honoured at the White House as one of President George Bush's "Daily Points of Light". Ms. Buchholz also serves on two committees as well as the advisory board for the Women's Sports Foundation.

As a scholarship tennis player for the University of Arizona, Ms. Buchholz graduated magna cum laude with a degree in finance. Upon graduation, she turned professional and competed for three years on the women's professional tennis tour where she achieved a world ranking. She is currently working on a Master's of Business Administration (MBA) at the University of Colorado in Colorado Springs.

Kian Lam Toh

Dr. Kian Lam Toh is an Assistant Professor of the Department of Physical Education in the Faculty of Social Sciences at Hong Kong Baptist University in Hong Kong. Born and raised in Singapore, he received his Bachelor of Education degree in Physical Education at the National Taiwan Normal University, Taiwan in 1992. His Master of Science degree in Recreation Administration and PhD degree in Leisure Behaviour were obtained in 1994 and 1997 respectively, both from Indiana University, USA. His teaching focus includes various aspects of sport and recreation management such as marketing, human resource and financial management; theory and practice in physical education and recreation, and fitness and recreation for selected populations. His research interests include sport management competency and behavioural aspects of sport and recreation.

Donna Lopiano

Dr. Lopiano is currently Executive Director of the Women's Sports Foundation. The Foundation, a national non-profit educational organisation, is among the top five grant-giving public women's funds in the United States, distributing over $1 million in grants to girls' and women's sports programs each year. Annually, the Foundation:

- Responds to over 100,000 requests for public information
- Distributes over 2 million pieces of educational materials
- Generates 1.5 billion media acknowledgements of its facts and opinions on women's sports issues
- Advocates in over 100 gender equity situations

According to The Sporting News, Lopiano is listed as #95 of the "100 Most Influential People in Sports" (2000) and Sports Business Journal lists her among the "top 10 female sports executives" in the nation. She received her Bachelor's degree from Southern Connecticut State University and her Master's and Doctoral degrees from the University of Southern California. She has been a college coach of men's and women's volleyball, and women's basketball, and softball. As an athlete, she participated in 26 national championships in four sports and was a nine-time All-American at four different positions in softball, a sport in which she played on six national championship teams. She is a member of the National Sports Hall of Fame, the National Softball Hall of Fame and the Texas Women's Hall of Fame among others. A prolific writer and speaker, she is considered by most to be a champion of equal opportunity for women in sport and the ethical conduct of educational sports.

Annie Clement

Dr. Annie Clement, who has a PhD from The University of Iowa and a J.D. from Cleveland State University, is an Associate Professor in the Sport

Administration program at Florida State University (Tallahassee, Florida). She is the author of *Law in Sport and Physical Activity* and *Legal Responsibility in Aquatics*; co-author of *The Teaching of Physical Skills* and *Equity in Physical Education*; and author of eleven book chapters and seventy-five articles.

Clement, who has given over one hundred presentations, is past president of the National Association for Sport and Physical Education and the Ohio Teacher Educators; Fellow of the American Bar Association, an award given to one third of one percent of ABA membership; and a member of the Ohio Bar and United States District Court, Northern District of Ohio.

Before joining FSU in 1998, Clement was at Cleveland State University where she was a Professor in the Sport Management program and a part-time lecturer in the College of Law. Dr. Clement has served in many different capacities throughout her years of teaching, advising, and administration. She has been a junior and senior high school teacher and coach, college teacher and coach, director of a sport management program, collegiate department chair, academic planner in a university vice-president's office, and associate dean of a college of education.

Paul Pedersen

Dr. Paul Pedersen was born in Stratton, Nebraska. He graduated from East High School (Pueblo, Colorado) in 1988. He continued his education at Palm Beach Atlantic College (West Palm Beach, Florida) and graduated in December, 1992 with a Bachelor of Science in Business Administration. In December of the following year, Pedersen completed his Master of Arts in Communication from Emerson College (Boston, Massachusetts). He then attended the University of Central Florida (Orlando, Florida), where he completed his Master of Arts degree in American History (with an emphasis in Sport History) in May, 1997.

Pedersen, who is an Assistant Professor of Sport Management at Bowling Green State University (Bowling Green, Ohio), has a Ph.D. in Sport Administration from Florida State University (Tallahassee, Florida). While at FSU he served as a research assistant to Dr. Annie Clement and a teaching assistant in the Physical Education Department. Beyond his academic pursuits, Dr. Pedersen has worked as a sports journalist and has taught courses in Sport Management, Communication, and the Mass Media at the college and university level. He is also the author of *Build it and they will come: The arrival of the Tampa Bay Devil Rays.*

THE BUSINESS OF SPORT

Editorial

Darlene Kluka & Guido Schilling

The International Council for Sport Science and Physical Education (ICSSPE), through its leadership, has determined a long-term publication's strategic plan to ensure success of endeavors such as this. Two years ago, members of the ICSSPE's Editorial Board envisioned a profound opportunity to expand the global *business of sport* knowledge base, utilizing a multi-disciplinary approach to the topic. The readership of this publication is as diverse as the content. Individuals representing governmental and non-governmental sport and sport science organizations, sport federations, universities and research institutes may benefit from this book. Representatives from the International Olympic Committee (IOC), United Nations Educational, Scientific, and Cultural Organization (UNESCO), World Health Organization (WHO), World Federation of the Sporting Goods Industry (WFSGI), and the General Assembly of International Sports Federations (GAISF) may also find it useful. Moreover, those with an interest in sport, sport science, and physical education, including teachers, coaches, and sport scientists, may also wish to apply its content toward the development of future leaders.

One of the fastest growing fields of endeavor, the *business of sport* has exploded worldwide, particularly within the last two decades. Although perspectives may vary, the *business of sport* is an issue that affects an enormous number of people in all sectors, at all levels, and in all areas of the globe.

Correspondence to: Dr. Darlene Kluka, Grambling State University, Dept. of HPER, P.O. 1193, Grambling, Louisiana, 71245, USA. Fax: +1 318 274 6053. E-mail: eyesport@windsong.net

One of the key features of the *Perspectives* Series is a global approach to a topic. Numerous authors have contributed chapters to provide a worldwide perspective on the *business of sport*. Although each contribution is unique, the authors, collectively, provide a framework from which readers can build their own strategies for decision making success through the *business of sport*.

The history and development of sport management as a scientific discipline are offered by Klein and Jones, where historical underpinnings and future possibilities are unveiled to the reader. The development and role of sport administrators in the success of sport management as a profession are detailed by Stier. The contributions and impact of sport in nation building is shared through the case of South Africa by Hendricks, while Toh provides a perspective on the role of sport in Asia, integrating traditional and contemporary paradigms in Hong Kong, China. The role and impact of athletes and sport agents on the professionalization of sport are presented by Clement and Pedersen, focusing on several perspectives that have begun to revolutionize the emerging sport agent job market. Cheek offers an inside look at the National Football League from a support team perspective, discussing the behind-the-scenes efforts that contribute to professional sport success. Lopiano discusses the contributions and impact of women on sport, perceived barriers, bridges, and infinite possibilities. Buchholz provides the framework for incorporating the constructs of volunteerism and professional staff in the administration of thousands of sport programs. Sport's contribution and impact to tourism and local economies are emphasized by Chalip, with insights into specific characteristics for success. Green spotlights multisport event management and its contributions as a medium in overall community development. An Asian corporate model of sport is configured by Masaru, whereby sport and business have been successfully partnered with communities.

Another key feature is the inclusion of a two-tier bibliography at the end of each chapter. Both have been designed to facilitate the search for general information, as evidenced by each initial bibliography. More in-depth information can be discovered through the use of resources available in the second bibliography. An additional resource in this *Perspectives* volume is a detailed list of books, journals, articles, and Internet sites for prospective sport administrators.

Finally, as editors, it is *our perspective* that success through sport is inspired by the strengths of many. Our collective commitment to the creation of a worldwide *business of sport* environment in which people can do their best, where goals can be ethically achieved, where differences are respected and valued, and where behaviors are assessed based upon systemic thinking and vision, integrity, courage, commitment, discipline, persistence, durability, people development, teamwork, communication, and the pursuit of excellence is pivotal for those who will be touched by the *business of sport*.

THE FUTURE OF SPORT BUSINESS

More Than Just A Game

Dion Klein and Don Jones

"Sport organizations which are not positioned appropriately to anticipate both the new challenges and the opportunities will be swamped by the onrushing waves of change within society. They can ill afford an attitude of 'business as usual'."
(Trenberth & Collins, 1994, p. 277)

Introduction

In 1994, Trenberth & Collins warned sports organizations about changes in the sports industry. Other writers in sport management have also projected this message (Thoma & Chalip, 1996; Van Der Smissen, 1991; Hillary Commission, 2000). The rate of change has increased immeasurably with the age of the Internet and other telecommunication advances. Along with this rate of change also comes an increasing amount of information practitioners and academics within the sports industry must consume in order to keep current with theory and practice.

Technology (including the Internet, broadband communication channels and digital television) will directly and indirectly impact everything we do in the future. It will change how we market products and services, how we educate, how we obtain funds and even how watch the game. This is only one of the twelve factors that have been identified that will impact the future of sports business.

Correspondence to: Dr. Dion Klein, Managing Director, Diverse Concepts International, P.O. Box 981, Belconnen, ACT 2616 Australia. Tel./Fax: +61 2 6287 4378. E-mail: drdionk@hotmail.com or Don Jones, Manager, Industry Development, Sport Industry Australia. E-mail: don@sportforall.com.au

Changing Definitions

> *Sport is "all forms of physical activity which, through casual or organised participation, aim at expressing or improving physical fitness and mental well-being, forming social relationships, or obtaining results in competition at all levels."*
> (The Council of Europe, 1992)

The definition of sport must be re-evaluated. Few programs will cater to the elite athlete; other programs will focus on healthy physical activity where the win-loss column will not be important. There are programs generating out of the sport sector in countries such as Australia, Singapore, and New Zealand that focus on physical activity rather than traditional competitive sport. These programs – Australia's *Active Australia*, New Zealand's *Push Play*, and Singapore's *Sport for All*, to name a few – incorporate the components of sport, physical activity, fitness and health. Depending on the country, sport may take the definition of elite, semi-amateur/professional sport, organized sport participation for the general population and healthy physical activity. For example, in South Africa, organized leisure sports are still a rarity. If organized sport does occur, it is in the sports of boys football and girls netball. Understanding the emphasis and scope of the market will become an increasingly important aspect in the business of sport.

Towards another slant, Alvin Toffler, in his famous book *Future Shock* published in 1970, highlighted 'fun specialists'. Back then he stated that people were creating not only various types of work, but play as well. We can see this in the increasing number of extreme sports that have emerged such as skateboarding, mountain biking, snowboarding, combat sport and paintball. As Toffler continued to note, "we shall advance into an era of breathtaking fun specialization – much of it based on sophisticated technology" (p. 256). That time has arrived.

Challenge: How do we want sport defined in 2010?

Market Waves

> *"Changing demographic, technological, time and economic pressures are redefining Australian sporting and recreation needs and activities"*
> (Rate, 1999, p. 4)

Rate's statement is applicable to the global marketplace. In no other time throughout history have so many demands been made upon us with the balance between work, play, and family becoming a challenge for everyone.

Sports marketers and managers will have to be aware of how these pressures will effect game and event attendance and the consumer's purchasing habits as well as the effect technology has on the spectator attendance. Convenience will become a very important factor in consumer decision-making since time will seem of the essence for many. Sports marketers will also have to be aware of the multicultural influence and the racial diversity of the marketplace which can have an effect on sport and physical activity participation and spectatorship. Other noticeable market factors will have to be considered.

The greyer market
The workforce is aging. There will be more consumer focus on the mature (over-55) age group. This group will focus more on health products and various forms of recreation and entertainment. (Kotler, 2000)

The children's market
As noted by Booth & Tatz (2000), the whole structure of children's sport depends on parents' time, money and emotion which are functions of economic class and social status. "Among the lower-income classes, money is a scarce resource and children's sport is often unaffordable. Children's sport is expensive: money is essential for equipment, uniforms, travelling, medical care, competition fees, club memberships and coaching. Most parents spend over $1000 per sport per year; many spend between $2000 and $3000. And the expenses rise dramatically if the child represents the region or state." (p. 200)

Not only do we have to be aware of the parent's time in transporting the children to practice and events, but children's time seems to become more competitive due their increased involvement not only in sport but also in dance and music. Additionally, some children are now avoiding organized sport due to poor body image (obesity is on the rise) as well as the pressures to win at all costs (usually from the parents or coach).

The widening gap between rich and poor
Despite the lessening communication gap between people due to the nature of telecommunications, the gap is widening between the rich and the poor. More companies are clearly targeting their products and services at either the high-income or low-income class. The middle class is slowly fading away.

The changing nature of family
There are more single-parent families, commuter families (i.e. one parent lives in a different city and commutes on weekends) and single households than before. This has an effect on what and when to offer the sport experience as well as the possible increased demand for child care facilities. Another influence on the changing nature of the family is the disposable income of gays and lesbians. In Australia, gays and lesbians contributed approximately AUS$1.1 billion to Australia's leisure and recreation industry – worth AUS$12 billion per annum.

The changing value of work and leisure
There is an increased blurring of work and play, and home and office (Anonymous (b), 2000). Though more people may be working longer hours (the typical "9-to-5" is rarely existent), the hours they keep may be different (i.e., flexible working hours, job sharing, telecommuting, etc.). Also, more people are opting for part-time or casual work or venturing into the entrepreneurial world, establishing a home-based business (Salzman, 2000). Due to technology and the opportunity to telework, sport businesses will have to market their services to these workers of the world (Cornish, Wagner, Johnson & Minerd, 2000). This can have an effect on sports-related businesses, such as hours of opening for retail, the times to offer organized sports competition and physical activity and access to such products and services. Sports that have not responded to the changing needs of the market will lose clients.

> *Challenge*: What strategies need to be developed to keep current with the changing needs of society?

Knowledge Capital

"We can seek to do better and better at what we are doing now – or we can change the way we do something. As a student, Fosbury did not seek to get better and better at the traditional Western-roll method of high jump. Instead he invented the Fosbury flop, which is a different approach. He won the Olympic high jump and changed the method for ever."
(de Bono, 1999, p. 128)

New management models are forming to move away from the *strategy-structure-systems* approach towards a more *purpose-process-people* approach (Anonymous (a), 2000). Educators must continually be aware of what knowledge, skills and attributes are needed by employers and whether they seek individuals with diverse or specialized skills. As indicated by Watt (1998), it is important that "sports administrators learn from more general management thinkers and their potential view of the future" (p. 222).

In the future, potential employees will have a business, finance, e-commerce and technology background as well as marketing, sponsorship and fundraising skills and experience. There are other practical skills that need to be learnt, such as effective communication skills (both oral and written) not only with someone from one's own country but other countries as well. Discipline, stress-management techniques, and wit have been cited as "critical components of successful careers" (Clarke, 2000). People will be hired more for their business acumen rather than their knowledge of the game.

There is also more competition to train future sports administrators and managers due to the on-line opportunities, private training companies and degree programs being outsourced to practitioners, including top executives, not only to save money, but also to add credibility to 'practical' areas for future employment. By having top executives teach parts of the program, business knowledge and experience is shared and the students have the opportunity to become better acquainted with the emerging business leaders in sport (Anonymous (a), 2000).

> *Challenge*: How can the sport industry adapt to the need for the investment in knowledge capital of both organizational and human resources to continuous improvement and lifelong learning?

Minority Forces

More 'minorities' are entering the sport industry workforce and there will be a stronger support network. Anti-discrimination policies will enforce that all people are created and treated equal.

As we enter into a more tolerant era where differences become more blurred between people with regard to their gender, race, sexual orientation, marital status, cultural background, etc., the typical 'old boys network' will slowly fade away. There will still be pockets that will have a very strong and very alive old boys network (probably from tradition), but the network will be challenged. For example, the Australian Football League recently appointed Elaine Canty to the AFL Board. This position used to be a token position for females, but now females are being nominated to the Board for their merit and capabilities. Other networks will emerge, physically and virtually, that will be much stronger with key role models acting as distant mentors.

"It is also anticipated that due to compensating technology, blindness, deafness, paralysis and other physical conditions will no longer be considered disabilities any more than nearsightedness is today" (Cornish, Wagner, Johnson & Minerd, 2000). This will allow a much easier transition for not only the employee, but also for the employer to sports industry positions.

The sport industry, like other sectors, must learn to operate in an environment that embraces social justice issues such as discrimination, equal opportunity, health and safety, privacy and child protection. Organizations and clubs, even those unincorporated, will need to understand and implement federal and state legislative requirements in order to avoid costly litigation for failure to comply.

> *Challenge*: How can organizations and clubs deal with the legal minefield of social justice issues?

The Bottom Line

> *"In no previous time period have we seen the type of growth in the commercialisation of sport, that we have seen in the last two decades"* (Slack, 1998).

Today large sums of money are involved in the transactions of sport, which has driven sport to be run as a business and be more accountable. We now have business relationships as well as sporting relationships. In transitioning from government-based sport to privately-owned or corporate sport, one must be aware that it is not so much what you have done or who you have met during the week, but how much money you have generated. Despite the amounts of money involved and the corporate nature of sport, one cannot forget the grassroots level. Employees and volunteers cannot feel alienated when the top end of sports enters into the corporate level.

In some countries such as Australia, Scotland, and England, where there is a strong volunteer base to operate sports organizations at the local and state (and sometimes national) level volunteers may feel negative towards hearing sport is now a business. In the purest business sense, when a company turns a profit, the profit goes back to the stakeholders and owners. In sport, when there is a 'profit' from a volunteer based organization, the money goes back into the organization to run more programs, buy equipment or add human resources. Watt (1998) stated it quite well relating the saying *'Think globally, act locally'* to sport suggesting that sport "must take into account the wider picture when putting together the practicalities of sport on a local basis where it has a real impact" (p. 223). So even though it may not be feasible or even applicable to operate sport as a business, the organization still needs to be run in a more business-like manner.

Challenge: How can the local sports club or state based organizations turn around the dependency on benevolent government funding and develop alternatives to the bottom line and self support?

Funding Challenges

"The Nike National League's GE Clubs are taking on the VISA American League's Chevrolet Boston Red Sox. Each inning is sponsored by a consumer food product, the game's most valuable player by Gillette, and the winning pitcher award by Radio Shack. The winning home run sets off a high-tech spectacular, courtesy of Microsoft, featuring virtual reality fireworks."
(Williams, 1996, p. 170).

In the future, sports marketing, sponsorship and advertising will be pushed to its limit. What happens when you run out of places to put logos and advertisements? Also, where do the smaller, not-as-financially-lucrative sports fit into the financial picture? There will be increased competition for sponsorship and funding for sport. There are sites now offering services for those seeking sponsorship information and opportunities on the Internet (e.g. <www.sponsorsonline.com>).

According to a study by SRI's European Sponsorship Monitor (1999), sport still leads the way in the number of sponsorship deals. The findings showed that sport sponsorship accounted for 68% of all deals in 1999, and 86% of their total value. Arts/culture was a distant second at 9.3% of their total value (Sportfacts, 2000). Despite the positive outlook for businesses still investing in sport, the competition for their dollar will be high and companies will expect a measurable return on investment (ROI). Also, "many companies will differentiate themselves by seriously sponsoring high-consensus social causes which then builds a civic character to increase the public's interest, respect and loyalty" (Kotler, 2000). Sport businesspeople need to consider innovative ways of fundraising campaigns to attract "something for nothing".

> *Challenge:* How will sport justify its return on investment and social cause?

Show Me the Money

> *"Athletes in the major spectator sports are marketable commodities, sports teams are traded on the stock market, sponsorship rights at major events can cost millions of dollars, network television stations pay large fees to broadcast games, and the merchandising and licensing of sporting goods is a major multi-national business."*
> (Slack, 1998)

In the movie *Jerry McGuire*, fading professional football star Rod Tidwell, played by actor Cuba Gooding, Jr., coined the phrase "Show me the money" that has become something of a 'catch-cry' for the cynical and shallow ethos of the late 1990's. It also reflects the increased Machiavellian behaviour of professional athletes to derive tangible financial benefits from their sporting prowess.

Up until the latter part of this century, money and sport were considered "wholly incompatible". Jim Thorpe was stripped of his 1912 Olympic gold medals because it was discovered that he was once paid to play baseball in his youth. The reasoning was that money would corrupt the sport's purity. In the past 20 years we have seen how money has impacted sport – Olympic scandals, bribery, illegal sports betting and game fixing – to name a few.

Money is powerful. That token of power can be used negatively or positively. The symbol of money does not wait until we become mature young adults either. In American Samoa, children will hesitate to play organized club sport unless there is a financial reward at the end of the season.

Sporting talent is at a premium, with its commercial value being recognized by the size of the salaries and endorsement deals signed by the leading performers (Roberts(a), 2000). The influence of agents has become more pronounced due to the inflationary salaries, the international labour market, and the growth in the players' intellectual property rights. For example, Australian professional rugby players are being lured by financially lucrative clubs in England to play for better salaries and opportunities. Australian Olympic medallist and champion 400m sprinter Cathy Freeman was embroiled in a court battle with her former manager over access to her money in the shape of Catherine Freeman Enterprises.

In the United States, 25-year old and All-Star baseball player Alex Rodriguez signed a record breaking new 10-year, $242 million contract with the Texas Rangers. The historic contract will earn the second-baseman an average of $25 million per year. The contract doubles the previous record for a sports contract when NBA forward Kevin Garnett and the Minnesota Timberwolves agreed to a US$126 million, 6-year contract in 1997.

Many athletes are high income earners and seek professional assistance on a fee for service basis for coaching, training, support services, sponsorship, publicity, management and investment. Most professional athletes are a small business in themselves.

> *Challenge:* How long will sport keep expanding – producing ever bigger salaries for players, more lucrative sponsorships, endorsements and television/broadcasting rights – before the bubble bursts?

Sportainment

Sport has always been a form of entertainment but now it is seeing its scope as a form of sports tourism (including sport fantasy vacations and event tourism), legalized sports gambling and publications dedicated to the sport entertainment industry. In the June 2000 issue, *Sport Business* announced its unique publishing joint venture with *Variety* (the leader in entertainment news) to establish a publication that "will focus on the development of sport as mainstream entertainment and as key content in the broadcaster's battle for ratings." (Where two worlds meet, 2000, p. 8)

Sport managers need to think creatively about new ways to package sport with travel opportunities. Belgian data suggested that the demand for sport as part of the travel experience increased 1300% over the past twenty years. Even low profile markets can capitalize such as Queensland Australia's scuba instruction industry earning over AUS$50 million per year to the State's economy (Chalip, 1995). The Internet has increased the travel industry's economic impact. By 2002, the largest e-commerce market will be travel, worth US$11.7 billion (Lyons, 2000). The implications of this are that sports adventure tours and fantasy vacations will be well placed on the Internet – but the competition will be high.

The Internet has also opened the doors to another entertainment industry – sports betting. One sports-betting company expects that online international wagering will grow from US$625 million in 1999, to approximately US$11 billion in 2004 (Armitage, 2000).

> *Challenge:* How will sport business professionals keep sport as entertainment without losing the essence of the game?

Megaplexes

One of the growing businesses of the sport industry will be facilities, primarily the mega-stadium. These massive stadiums will be able to accommodate any sport, entertain major convention-goers, have hydraulic lifts to move floors and seating – the limit is unknown. A few of these stadia were featured in *Sports Technology* (1998) including Stade de France (Paris), Docklands Stadium (Melbourne, Australia) and Stadium Australia (Sydney), home of the Opening and Closing Ceremonies of the 2000 Olympic Games. It will be imperative for sport businesspeople to understand the technology of building the stadiums and the implications it can have on the programming and management of the facility. With a world wide trend to the building of multipurpose sport and leisure centres, which cater for all levels of users, the need for effective facility management is a financial imperative.

Challenge: Which will take priority – having a pure background of facility management with an understanding of business or vice versa?

Partnerships

There will be an even greater emphasis on establishing networks and affiliations in the future – but they will be different from the past. There will be more need to have affiliations and partnerships with non-sport-related companies such as travel, hospitality business product and service suppliers. Lachowetz (personal communication, July 5, 2000) discussed the concept of "regional sports alliances" and the positive outcomes of particular sports working together that occupied a geographic region. There is greater opportunity to develop partnerships, alliances, and networks via the Internet as we see in the power of on-line communities, cultures and vertical portals being developed in sport (Clark, 2000; Notess, 2000).

Globalization

We have seen how telecommunications have affected the fluctuation in the global economy, but overall the global economy is positive. The development of telecommunications and technology has lessened the global gap. The benefits of globalization are huge.

Many businesses are now exporting products and services (including sport education), and the Internet makes it even easier in today's world. Sport has an opportunity to participate in the approximate US$7 trillion world export of goods and services which is anticipated to top US$11 trillion by 2005 (Cornish, Wagner, Johnson, & Minerd, 2000). Australian exports of sport and recreation goods was estimated at AUS$371 million in 1997-98. Australian Sport International's export target, after piggy-backing off the Sydney Olympic Games, is US$1.3 billion by 2006. It must also be highlighted that "the reality of a global marketplace places increased pressures on businesses in areas such as specialization, product differentiation for particular markets, lead times from development to product launch, and economies of scale." (DISR, 1999, p. 6)

> *Challenge:* How will sport continue to capitalize on the globalization of the industry?

Going Digital

> *"IOC President Juan Antonio Samaranch has admitted that sport federations are 'lost' when it comes to forming a coherent internet strategy. ... At the moment we are lost. We have big worries about what can happen in the future, not only for the IOC but also sports federations."*
> (Samaranch, 2000, p. 1)

The Internet is still new to sport. In 1999, only 36% of Americans had used the Internet for sports information; more than 10 million adults stated they watched television while on the Internet with 24% of them showing sports events (Gellatly, 2000). It is estimated by 2004, e-commerce related to sports will be approximately US$5 billion.

There is a plethora of Internet sites dedicated to sports in the form of business-to-business portals (www.b4bsport.com.au), business-to-consumer portals (www.sportnet.com.au; www.thesportsauthority.com), community-building sites (www.eosports.com), and text based information services (such as on-line journals, etc.). Internet technology is becoming more advanced. For example, for the 2000 Olympic games, IBM's website included real-time scoring and results, play-by-play commentary, and webcam images of eleven sports.

Another technology that has already made an appearance is broadband Internet/telecommunication channels which "will allow people to get high speed access to the Net, fast and instantaneous access to information, and constant access without having to log on and off..." (Lyons, 2000, p. 10). Sport has the opportunity to be at the forefront utilizer of the technology.

Another technology is Worldzap, a device that "will deliver sports (and music) content to the world via a new generation of mobile telephone devises capable of displaying quality pictures as well as text" (Roberts (b), 2000, p. 54). The implications of this are phenomenal, from a marketing point of view, especially when integrated with digital sponsorship technology (e.g., www.symah-vision.fr).

Britcher (2000) sees the future as being dynamic for broadcasters to embrace the technology, and leagues and federations to discover a new revenue source, which will not interrupt the action on the field. "The way we view sport is set to improve rapidly as we move further into the new century. With the potential of the Internet as well, it appears there really may be no limit to what could be achieved" (p. 23).

Another principal challenge for today's sports administrator is to keep up with the changing face of applied technology in the sport industry. The application of technology has continued to advance the cutting edge of sport, particularly in the fields of exercise physiology and sports biomechanics. A simple example of the heart-rate monitor and portable blood lactate testing devices, once the mainstay of scientific laboratory procedures, are now readily available and typically part of the athlete's routine daily training kit. In field hockey, the use of video-analysis of pre-recorded opposition plays, with real-time download capability has complemented the application of game strategy for coaching purposes. For example, a type of penalty corner set-up may be counteracted with a set defense.

> *Challenge:* How will we prepare future sports administrators and managers to embrace and understand the rapid technological developments when sport (as a whole) is only grasping how to be business like?

Summary

> *'Everything is fine. But the ship is still heading in the wrong direction.'*
> (de Bono, 1999, p. 1)

Sport needs to evaluate where it thinks it is, where it really is, where it thinks it is heading, and where it really is heading. It goes deeper than just developing a three-year strategic plan. The world is changing too rapidly to where a 6-month operational plan is more realistic and feasible.

This list is definitely not all inclusive of factors that the sport businessperson needs to take into consideration to operate one's organization. The professional sports manager, leader, and administrator needs to be aware of what is happening in many more sectors than in previous times. We are fortunate in this age that we do have easier access to this information because of the Internet. The times ahead will not only be challenging but exciting.

Lastly, the Australian Sports Commission noted this in its 1998-2001 Strategic Plan, "...Sport may be increasingly commercially developed by entrepreneurs with little attention to the once dominant amateur ideology" (DISR, 1999, p. 22). It's more than just a game – it's business.

rea.

References

Anonymous (a). (2000, February). Creating a university to train tomorrow's leaders. *HR Focus* [On-line]. Available: <http://global.umi.com>

Anonymous (b). (2000, April/June). 10 trends shaping the decade. *Competitive Intelligence Magazine* [On-line]. Available: <http://global.umi.com>

Armitage, L. (2000, April 8). All bets are off in the Assembly's looming battle over licenses for online casinos. *Canberra Times*, C1, C2.

Booth, D., & Tatz, C. (2000). *One-Eyed: A View of Australian Sport.* Sydney: Allen & Unwin.

Britcher, C. (2000, April). Enhancing the big picture. *Sport Business*, 23-24.

Chalip, L. (1995, November). *Sport: Is it a brave new world?* Paper presented for the ASSA Sport Management conference "The Business of Sport", Brisbane, Australia.

Clark, P. (2000, Jan/Feb). Top trends: Alliances, net growth key in 2000. *Advertising Age's Business Marketing* [On-line]. Available: <http://global.umi.com>

Clarke, R. D. (2000, February). The future is now. *Black Enterprise* [On-line]. Available: <http://global.umi.com>

Cornish, E., Wagner, C., Johnson, D., & Minerd, J. (2000, Jan/Feb). Special report: The opportunity century – introduction. *The Futurist* [On-line]. Available: <http://global.umi.com>

de Bono, E. (1999). *New Thinking for the New Millennium.* London: Penguin Books.

Department of Industry, Sport and Resources (DISR). (1999). *End Goal 2006: Moving the sport and recreation industry to a higher growth path.* Canberra: Commonwealth of Australia.

Field of play. (1998). *Sports Technology*, 29-33.

Gellatly, A. (2000, June). Pausing in the rush to broadband, *Sport Business*, 15.

Hillary Commission. (2000, January). *Sport and Active Leisure: The*

Future Marketing Environment. A Hillary Commisson Discussion Paper. Available: <http://www.hillarysport.org.nz/pdfs/strategy/marketing.pdf>

Kotler, P. (2000, February). Future markets. Executive Excellence [On-line]. Available: <http://global.umi.com>

Lyons, K. (2000, March 17). 5 cybertrends driving e-business. *Emarketing and Internet Guide*, 6-11.

Notess, G.R. (2000, Jan/Feb). On the net in 2000. *Online* [On-line]. Available: <http://global.umi.com>

Rate, Y. (1999, Nov/Dec). Challenges for the new millennium. *Activate*, 4-6.

Roberts (a), K. (2000, April). Sport's growing wealth of riches. *Sport Business*, p. 29.

Roberts (b), K. (2000, April). WAP's world of possibilities. *Sport Business*, 54.

Salzman, M. (2000, March 1). The future of work. *CIO* [On-line]. Available: <http://global.umi.com>

Samaranch calls for techno summit. (2000, June). *Sports Business*, 1.

Slack, T. (1998). Studying the commercialisation of sport: The need for critical analysis. *Sociology of Sport Online* [On-line]. Available: <http://www.brunel.ac.uk/depts/sps/sosol/v1i1a6.htm>

The Council of Europe. (1992, September 24). *European Sports Charter*.

Toffler, A. (1970). *Future Shock*. London: The Bodley Head.

Thoma, J.E., & Chalip, L. (1996). *Sport Governance in the Global Community*. Morgantown, WV: Fitness Information Technology.

Trenberth, L, & Collins, C. (1994). *Sport Management in New Zealand: An Introduction*. Palmerston, New Zealand: Dunmore Press.

Van der Smissen, B. (1991). Future directions. In Parkhouse, B. (ed.), *The Management of Sport: Its Foundation and Application* (pp. 381-404). Chicago: Mosby.

Watt, D. (1998). *Sports Administration and Management*. London: E & FN Spon.

Where two worlds meet. (2000, June). *Sports Business*, 8.

Williams, R.M. (1996). The future of sports marketing. In McCormack, M. (ed.), *Mark McCormack's Guide to Sports Marketing* (pp. 170-176). Largo, FL: International Sports Marketing Group.

Bibilography for Non-Specialists

Andrews, J. (1998, June 6). Survey: The world of sport: The paymasters. *The Economist* [On-line]. Available: <http://global.umi.com>

Baird, B. (1997, October). *The impact of the growing sports Industry on the Australian tourism market.* Paper presented for the Australia in the World Sports Marketplace conference, Sydney, Australia.

Galvin, N. (2000, June 10-16). Virtual spectators. *Sydney Morning Herald*, p. 4-5.

Glendinning, M. (2000, June). Special agents licensed to ring the tills. *Sport Business*, 10-11.

Hannan, G. (1997, October). *Is the Australian sports industry heading down the same road as the USA?* Paper presented for the Australia in the World Sports Marketplace conference, Sydney, Australia.

Prince, C.J. (2000, April). E-business: A look at the future. *Chief Executive* [On-line]. Available: <http://global.umi.com>

Sky gets SIG for $550m. (2000, June). *Sport Business*, 3.

Sportfacts. (2000, April). *Sports Business*, 58.

Thames, R. (2000, March). Pursue e-business or die. *Strategic Finance* [On-line]. Available: <http://global.umi.com>

The Sports Administration Revolution. (1995, September). *Sports Rap: Newsletter of the New Zealand and Sports Foundation, Inc.*, 2.

SPORT MANAGEMENT

The Development of Sport Management

William F. Stier, Jr.

Introduction

The sport world has undergone tremendous changes in recent years - both in terms of the number and scope of sport activities available to the populace and in terms of the number of people involved, in some aspect, with sport activities and the business of sport. As a result, sport and the conduct of sport related activities and organizations have become more complex and more challenging than ever before. To have a better appreciation of the world of sport as it exists today, and as it might exist in the future, it is helpful to view sports and sport activities from several different points of view as shown in Figure 1 on the following page.

First, there is the recreational (leisure time) or competitive aspect of sport. Is a particular sport activity essentially a recreational experience (even if it involves competitive aspects)? Or, is the sport experience truly competitive in nature? Second, one may examine the financial base and support of a sport. Is the sport activity part of a non-profit organization (a public or municipal entity, or a school, for example)? Or, is the sport sponsored a for-profit venture (professional sports teams, etc.). Third, sport may be viewed from the vantage point of spectators as well as participants. Fourth, the world of sport may be conceptualized to include health, fitness and wellness activities and programs organized and sponsored by both private groups or associations and by public organizations.

Correspondence to: Dr. William Stier, Jr., Professor and Graduate Director, Physical Education & Sport, State University of New York, Brockport, NY 14420, USA. Tel: +1 716 395 5331 Fax: +1 716 395 2771. E-mail: bstier@brockport.edu

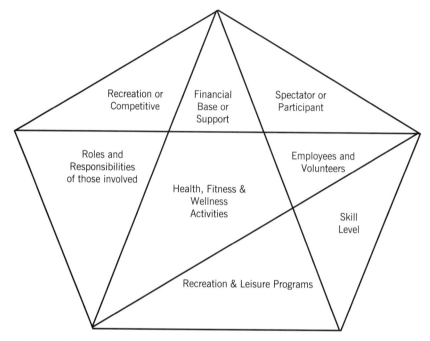

Figure 1: The Different Perspectives of Sport

Fifth, there is a matter of how workers in the sport programs are compensated, that is, whether they are paid employees or serve as volunteers. Sixth, there is the aspect of the different levels of skills associated with competitive or recreational sport activities for people of different ages. For example, sport activities may be made available at the youth level, within schools (secondary and university levels), municipal/city programs, Olympic competition, semi-professional sports, as well as the world of professional sports. Lastly, sports may be examined from the vantage point of the managerial roles and administrative responsibilities of those individuals who are involved in some part of the sport program.

The Business of Sport

Having an understanding of sports in light of the seven factors listed above helps one to understand and appreciate the complicated and sophisticated world of both recreational and competitive sports in our society. Because of the expansion of sport today (and in the future) coupled with the tremendous increase in the number of people involved with sport, the process of planning, organizing and implementing sport activities and sport programs has become so involved and so sophisticated that it requires highly skilled, well-trained, educated – as well as experienced – individuals to be consistently successful in administering and managing sport today.

More and more sports and sport programs have come to be viewed as a business or business related (even if non-profit) because of (1) the size and sophistication of the programs themselves, (2) the impact that such programs can have upon individuals, communities, organizations, and society itself, (3) the complexity involved in the planning, management and administration of sports; and, (4) the resources (money, effort and time) needed to conduct quality sport programs at almost every level, from the youth or elementary level to the professional level. This is true regardless of whether the sports are sponsored by non-profit or for-profit entities.

The Art and Science of Sport Management

The management of sport may be considered both a science and an art. It is a science in that there are fundamental principles, concepts and a body of knowledge underlying and supporting the tasks associated with managing and administering any sport activity or sport program. These principles and concepts are applicable in any number of situations and under varying circumstances - they generally hold true regardless of the setting in which the sport manager finds oneself in. For example, many of these principles are applicable whether one is engaged in the business of manufacturing sports, recreation or leisure products, in the business of providing services in sport, recreation, or leisure activities, or in the business of providing opportunities or services for spectators and/or participants at various sport, recreation, or leisure programs or activities.

However, sport management may also be considered an art since the implementation of the administrative techniques and managerial strategies and tactics can be significantly affected, and in many instances enhanced, through the creative and innovative utilization of these principles and the application of the knowledge pertaining to management (Stier, 1999, p. 6). Thus, how one goes about actually managing sport and making decisions relating to the management of sport is dependent upon one's personality and attitude, prior experiences, and one's creativity in the decision making process.

The Beginning of the Formal Preparation of Sport Managers

To manage and administer the ever-growing and increasingly more complex sport programs in our society requires specially trained and educated individuals. These individuals must understand both the role of sport in our society and the concepts and principles of management as they pertain to administering sport programs in any number of venues and under different circumstances, situations and limitations. The availability of such highly educated sport managers, specifically trained and knowledgeable in the business of managing and administering sports and sport programs, became a reality shortly after an American university, Ohio University (Athens), implemented the first professional preparation program in 1966.

Dr. James G. Mason, known as the "Father of Sport Management", was the person responsible for starting the first formal educational program in sport management in 1966 (Photo 1). This initial program was offered exclusively at the master's level. The impetus for this program began a decade earlier (1957) when Walter O'Malley, who was then the president of the Brooklyn Dodgers baseball team, voiced a concern to Dr. Mason, then a professor of Physical Education at the University of Miami, about the lack of any formal educational programs for individuals desiring to work in professional sports, specifically, professional baseball (Stier, 1999). It took Dr. Mason, who subsequently moved to Ohio University, almost a decade to create the first sport management program that was part of a university curriculum (J.G. Mason, Personal Communication, May 6, 1997).

Photo 1: Dr. James G. Mason – "The Father of Sports Management"

Rapid Expansion of Educational Institutions Offering Sport Management Programs

From this humble beginning in 1966, the growth of college and university based educational programs in sport management has been explosive. The University of Massachusetts instituted the second graduate program in 1971. This was followed a year later by the third such program which was initiated by Western Illinois University. The first graduate program at an Historically Black College or University (HBCU) was established in 1974, at Grambling State University of Louisiana. In less than six years, there were 20 sport management programs in the United States (Parkhouse, 1978). In addition, three undergraduate sport management programs had also been established during this time period at Biscayne College (now St. Thomas University) in Miami, Florida, the State University of New York (Brockport), and at St. John's University (New York) (Stier, 1993).

The trend towards continual growth and expansion continued and in 1982, there were 44 graduate and undergraduate sport management programs in the United States alone (Lewis, 1982). And, six years later this number had jumped considerably to 58 graduate programs and 75 undergraduate programs (Sports, Inc., 1988).

The expansion of programs continued unabated and by 1993, there were 193 colleges and universities in the United States as well as 14 in Canada offering undergraduate and/or graduate programs in sport management and/or athletic administration (NASSM/NASPE, Sport Management, 1993).

By 1997, the United States had eight doctoral level programs preparing sport managers and administrators. These schools included (1) University of Connecticut, (2) Florida State University, (3) University of Iowa, (4) University of Massachusetts, (5) University of New Mexico, (6) University of Northern Colorado, (7) The Ohio State University; and, (8) the United States Sports Academy [Daphne, Alabama] (Stier, 1999, p. 13).

At the beginning of the second millennium it is estimated that over 250 undergraduate and graduate programs are in existence throughout the world. This rapid growth speaks to the need that is perceived for professionally prepared and knowledgeable sport managers and administrators, both now and in the future.

Reasons for the Explosive Growth of Sport Management Programs

There have been a number of different reasons given for the explosive growth of sport management programs over the past 35 years. Leaders in physical education departments initiated a majority of the early sport management programs. In fact, even today, in the United States the majority of such programs are housed in physical education (or kinesiology, sports studies or similar departments). In many instances, these leaders recognized that physical education was a broad based academic discipline and that sport management was a natural outgrowth of physical education and, in fact, was an integral part of its academic curriculum. In other instances, there were conscious efforts by physical education faculty to meet a real need for professionally trained managers within the broad context of sport and sport-related organizations by offering such programs within the umbrella of physical education.

This need for professionally trained sport managers is clearly evident when viewed in the light that "historically over 98% of all first time managers in all types of organizations are placed in their first supervisory jobs without being trained to manage first" (Bridges & Roquemore, 1992, p. 4). This practice, widespread in the world of sport, at all levels, is not only viewed as an unfortunate and deplorable situation, but it placed the well-being of the affected sport programs, as well as those involved in such programs, in an untenable position.

What is clearly needed is quality leadership, quality supervision, quality organization, quality guidance, and quality management of sport activities and sport programs - if the real potential of such activities and programs are to be realized in our society, now and in the future. Towards this end, many institutions of higher education have instituted sport management professional preparation programs with the goal of preparing skilled and experienced professionals to assume the reins of overseeing, planning, supervising and implementing quality sport programs.

Questionable Reasons for Instituting Sport Management Programs
However, although many sport management programs were established in response to a very real need for qualified, trained and experienced sport managers, it cannot be overlooked that, at least in some instances, such programs were established for more selfish reasons. For example, some sport management programs were instituted primarily in an effort to save jobs (i.e., to justify the existence of existing personnel) within those physical education departments where student enrolments were substantially decreasing (Stier, 1986). There have been more than a few institutions of higher education in which the primary rationale for initiating sport management programs was the blatant desire to maintain or increase student enrolment within that institution (and thus to save teaching jobs) - especially when other (competing) institutions showed significant increases in students seeking to pursue sport management at the college/university level.

Although the rationale behind the initiation of a sport management program may not have any direct influence on the eventual quality of the faculty and the academic integrity of the curriculum and the program in total, one cannot deny that there has been a very, very rapid expansion of the number of schools offering such sport management programs. Some in the profession believe that the proliferation of both undergraduate and graduate programs has not been altogether healthy for the profession, nor justified in light of the available job openings and career opportunities.

Problems with the Proliferation of Sport Management Programs
One of the consequences of having such a great number of colleges and universities offering sport management programs (undergraduate and/or graduate levels) is that there is a very real danger of unemployment and

underemployment in the area of sport management. In other words, there is a very real danger of saturating the job market with otherwise knowledgeable, highly trained, well educated and experienced sport management graduates, all competing for far too few vacancies. Whenever there is an oversupply of qualified personnel seeking a limited number of positions the possible consequences include (1) a low rate of pay, (2) unemployment, (3) underemployment; and, (4) a high turnover rate among workers who do find employment and who become dissatisfied with their future career options.

Components of the Educational Programs Preparing Sport Managers

Partially in response to the proliferation of undergraduate and graduate sport management programs, many in the profession have felt that there was a need to provide some level or degree of (minimal) quality assurance to students enrolling in programs and to the employers hiring graduates of these programs. As a result, there has been a movement within the profession to establish standards in terms of the content of professional preparation programs at colleges and universities in the form of voluntary standards (Schneider & Stier, 2000).

It was agreed that the so-called **program approval approach** was one that could help assure both students and potential employers alike that the graduates of approved sport management programs would have been adequately prepared in essential content areas to such an extent that the graduates would have appropriate knowledge, experience, skills and competencies to be effective and efficient professionals in the business world of sport. The overall goal was to provide an incentive for colleges and universities to upgrade their sport management professional preparation programs (undergraduate and graduate) in an attempt to meet these standards - thereby better preparing their students for entry into a variety of sport management careers (Stier & Schneider, 2000).

This effort became a reality in 1993 when the National Association for Sport and Physical Education (NASPE) and the North American Society for Sport Management (NASSM) published a document containing a list of minimum competency areas (essential core content areas) for sport management programs at both the undergraduate and graduate levels

(NASPE/NASSM Joint Task Force, 1993). In addition, the document also included a program approval protocol to evaluate programs for compliance with the standards (Sport Management Program Standards and Review Protocol, May 1993). In more recent years (1999), NASPE and NASSM sought to revise the undergraduate and graduate standards (essential content areas). At the time of this writing, the proposed revised undergraduate and graduate sport management curriculum core content areas are listed in Figure 2.

Undergraduate Content Areas	Graduate Content Areas
1. Socio-Cultural Dimensions in Sport	1. Socio-Cultural Dimensions in Sport
2. Management and Leadership in Sport	2. Management and Leadership in Sport
3. Ethics in Sport Management	3. Ethics in Sport Management
4. Marketing in Sport	4. Marketing in Sport
5. Communications in Sport	5. Communications in Sport
6. Budget and Finance in Sport	6. Financial Management in Sport
7. Legal Aspects of Sport	7. Legal Aspects of Sport
8. Economics in Sport	8. Research in Sport
9. Venue and Event Management in Sport	9. Venue and Event Management in Sport
10. Governance in Sport	10. Field Experience in Sport Management
11. Field Experience in Sport Management	

Figure 2: Proposed Revised Sport Management Curriculum Core Content Areas for Undergraduate and Graduate Programs

Components of a Modern Sport Management Curriculum.

The ultimate goal of a quality sport management curriculum (program) is to enable the student (graduate) to develop a high competency level in those skills and knowledge areas necessary in the business of sport in our society. These competencies include (1) the mastery of a specific body of knowledge, (2) being self-reliant and self-motivated, (3) being able and willing to continue to learn, (4) being capable of making proper and opportune adjustments in light of varying circumstances and situations, (5) being willing to assume reasonable risks, (6) being able to relate to and interact with others (individually and in groups); and (7) being capable and willing to make appropriate and timely decisions in critical situations.

Towards this end, all sport management curricula involve, to some extent, courses and learning experiences in the following four areas. First, there are general liberal arts courses, general education courses, which enable the individual to develop a well rounded, broad based, education. These courses are the foundation of a liberal arts education. Second, there are cognate or sport/management-linked courses. These are classes that are taught typically within a variety of departments within the university that are nevertheless related to the field of sport and sport management.

Third, there are specialty or major courses in sport management itself. These are the courses that comprise the sport management essential core content areas (Figure 2). These courses deal with the specific body of knowledge or subject matter that is sport management and are taught by experts trained in the subject matter of sport management and, ideally, who also possess real life experience in the business of sport and sport management.

The fourth area of formal education associated with sport management is commonly referred to as field experiences. These learning opportunities typically consist of real-life experiences in any number of sport management roles and positions and which expose the student to the real world of sport, the business of sport, and the management of sport. These field experiences can be (1) part-time stints assumed while still actively engaged in classroom work, typically called practica or observation-type experiences, or (2) full time involvements, usually referred to as internships. An internship is usually a terminal or concluding field experience, usually full time, and completed by the student after all course work is completed. The key to all successful and meaningful field experiences is providing the individual student with an early and accurate glimpse of what life as a sport management employee might be like and to enable the individual to assume responsibilities and to perform meaningful tasks commensurate with one's abilities, skills, experiences, and risk tolerance.

Job Opportunities for Sport Managers in the Business of Sport

Sport job opportunities have grown and matured significantly in recent years, both in terms of the number and type of positions that are available. Today, there are a wide variety of job opportunities in many sport and sport-related areas in our society for interested, motivated and qualified individuals. Job opportunities under the umbrella commonly referred to as sport management include positions in the areas of health, wellness and fitness as well as recreation and leisure time activities - in addition to the competitive sport arena.

With the ever increasing popularity (both by spectators and participants) of these sport related activities, at all levels of skill and among people of all ages, the opportunities for involvement, both on a paid and on a volunteer basis, will continue to grow. However, along with an expansion of job opportunities will be a corresponding increase in competition from others who will also seek to become engaged in some aspect of the business world of sport (Stier, 1998).

There are ten broad categories of sport and sport related job opportunities or career paths awaiting the sport management graduate. These include (1) media related positions, (2) manufacturing positions, (3) service and support positions, (4) marketing and promotional related positions, (5) fundraising, (6) self-employment and entrepreneurship opportunities, (7) managerial and administrative positions, (8) representative and agency involvements, (9) sales jobs; and (10) facility related posts.

Within these broad categories there are seemingly countless jobs or positions as well as types of organizations that aspiring men and women (sport managers) might successfully pursue in their search for a career opportunity within the business of what we refer to as *sport(s)*. These job positions or involvements include, but are not limited to, the following: athletic team management, finance, amateur sport agencies such as the NCAA, NAIA, AAU, etc., journalism, broadcasting, sports information, statistics and record keeping, care of equipment and supplies, sports medicine, sports training, public relations, sport merchandising, ticket sales, marketing, promotions, development and fundraising, facility management, home event organization, cardiovascular fitness and wellness management, sports medicine programs, corporate fitness administration, municipal recreation departments, armed services recreation and sports programs, sports commissions, non-profit sport organizations (YMCA/YWCA, CYO, Scouts, Boys/Girls Clubs, etc.), city/state sport commissions, federal parks and recreation programs, sport law opportunities including sport agents and sport agencies, league offices, conference commissioners' offices, hotel/resort recreation programs, theme parks, horse racing positions, car racing endeavors, aquatics/tennis/golf clubs, tourism, proprietary recreation businesses, i.e., "Discovery Zones", sport manufacturing (equipment and supplies), professional and semi-professional sport organizations, school sports, youth sports, educational/sports consultants, computer/web managers, specialized sport resorts, cruise opportunities, summer sport camps, specialized instructional sport programs, and sport service organizations, just to mention a few.

The Future of Sport Management

There are numerous challenges as well as opportunities facing sport management in the future. The fact that more and more individuals, who are involved in the training and educating of future sport managers, possess doctoral degrees in sport management is truly significant. The teachers (professors) of those students enrolled in the early sport management programs (both undergraduate and graduate) did not possess the terminal degree in sport management but were self-taught. This was because there were either none or very few doctoral programs in sport management for many years. Today, and in the future, this will drastically change as those early graduates of the sport management doctoral degree programs assume leadership roles in the teaching of future sport managers. The result will be an even greater degree of sophistication and competency of the graduates from more and more sport management programs at the graduate as well as the undergraduate level.

Since there will be more faculty members with the doctoral degree in sport management involved in the professional preparation of future sport managers, it is anticipated that the academic integrity and educational quality of the typical sport management curriculum as well as the overall learning experience for students will be substantially enhanced and improved. This new generation of sport management leaders and teachers will usher in an even greater degree of sophistication and quality in terms of future graduates of the sport management programs, both graduate and undergraduate.

In respect to the proliferation of schools offering sport management programs, there is a distinct possibility of a shakeout in terms of all of these same schools retaining such programs. This is due to the fact that sport management graduates produced today greatly outnumber the available quality job opportunities in the business world of sport. As a consequence, those schools unable or unwilling to offer a truly demanding, high calibre and sophisticated professional preparation program (up-to-date curriculum, modern facilities/equipment and quality faculty) – and to also attract high quality and motivated students – will be forced to leave the "playing field" of sport management to those institutions who are able to do these things.

Accompanying the upgrading of the schools offering sport management programs will be a continual expansion and increase in the skills, competencies and experiences of those individuals graduating from such programs and seeking employment in the business of sport. This enhancing of the competency level of sport managers, at all levels, will have a direct impact upon the quality level and sophistication in all areas and at every level of sport and sport programs - amateur and professional, recreational and competitive.

Another trend to watch for in the future will be closer cooperation (or in some instances, competition) between university and college schools/ departments of *business* and *physical education*. There is an increasing trend to house sport management in the business schools or departments, or, at the very least to forge some type of cooperative venture between the so-called physical education and the business departments, insofar as preparing future sport managers. This is in recognition of the fact that an important or essential element in sport management is that of business, the business of sport. As a result, it is anticipated that business departments and schools will seek to become more involved in the exciting world of sport management and the preparation of future sport mangers for the world of sport.

Conclusions

Sports have become big business today and will become even more so in the foreseeable future. In fact, revenues associated with sports in the United States alone, at the turn of the century, were estimated to exceed the $100-billion mark. The opportunities for the general populace in any country to become involved in some aspect, i.e., as a participant, spectator, employee, consumer, etc., will continue to expand exponentially. As a result, there will be an ever-present need for competent, professionally trained and experienced sport managers to assume leadership roles in the various and numerous sport businesses, organizations and programs (Stier, 1999, August 13).

References

Bridges, F.L., & Roquemore, L.L. (1992). *Management for athletic/sport administration: Theory and practice*. Decatur, GA: ESM Books.

Lewis, G. (1982). *Degree programs in athletic and sport administration*. Unpublished report, University of Massachusetts.

NASSM/NASPE. (1993, March). Sport management - Directory of professional preparation. North American Society for Sport Management (NASSM)/National Association for Sport and Physical Education (NASPE) Sport Management Task Force, Reston, VA: National Association for Sport and Physical Education.

NASSM/NASPE. (1993, May). *Sport management program standards and review protocol*. Reston, VA.

NASPE/NASSM Joint Task Force on Sport Management Curriculum and Accreditation. (1993, May). Standards for curriculum and voluntary accreditation of sport management education programs. *Journal of Sport Management, 1(3)*, 159-170.

Parkhouse, B.L. (1978). Professional preparation in athletic administration and sport management. *Journal of Physical Education, Recreation and Dance, 49(5)*, 22-27.

Schneider, R. & Stier, Jr., F. (2000). Sport Management Curricular Standards 2000 Study–Graduate Level. *International Journal of Sport Management, 1(2)*, 137-149.

Sports, Inc. (1988, May 23). *A class compendium*, 3.

Stier, Jr., W.F. (1986). Challenges facing physical education: Alternative career options. *Journal of Physical Education, Recreation and Dance, 57(8)*, 26-27.

Stier, Jr., W.F. (1993, August). *Alternative career paths in physical education: Sport management*. Washington, D.C. ERIC Digest - Clearinghouse on Teacher Education.

Stier, Jr. W.F. (1998). *Sport management: Career planning and professional preparation*. Boston, MA: American Press.

Stier, Jr., W.F. (1999). *Managing sport, fitness and recreation programs: Concepts and practices.* Needham Heights, MA: Allyn & Bacon.

Stier, Jr., W.F. (1999, August 13). *Fundamental concepts of fundraising, promotions, and public relations for the fitness/sport manager.* Paper presented at the 8th international convention of the National Sport Council of Taiwan (in Taipei City) organized by the Aerobic Fitness and Health Association of Taiwan. Sponsored by IHRSA and IDEA - Republic of China.

Stier, Jr., W.F., & Schneider, R. (2000). Sport Management Curricular Standards 2000 Study – Undergraduate Level. *International Journal of Sport Management, 1(1),* 56-59.

Non-Specialists Bibliography

Davis, K.A. (1994). *Sport management: Successful private sector business strategies.* Madison, WI: WCB Brown & Benchmark.

Graham, P.J. (1994). *Sport business: Operational and theoretical aspects.* Madison, WI: WCB Brown & Benchmark.

Horine, L. (1999). *Administration of physical education and sport programs* (4th ed.). Boston, MA: WCB McGraw-Hill.

Markiewiez, D.A. (1991, July 30). More fans line up for careers in sports. *USA Today,* 7-B.

Masteralexis, L.P., Barr, C.A., & Hums, M.A. (Eds.). (1998). *Principles and practice of sport management.* Gaithersburg, MD: Aspen Publishers, Inc.

Railey, J.H., & Tschgauner, P.R. (1993). *Managing physical education, and sports programs.* Mountain View, CA: Mayfield Publishing Company.

Sawyer, T.H., & Smith, O. (1999). *The management of clubs, recreation and sport: Concepts and applications.* Champaign, IL: Sagamore Publishing.

Sports, Inc. (1988, May 23). *A class compendium,* p. 3.

Stier, Jr., W.F. (1994). *Successful sport fund-raising.* Madison, WI: WCB Brown & Benchmark.

Stier, Jr., W.F., & Schneider, R. (1999). Fundraising: An essential competency for the sports manager in the 21st century. *The Mid-Atlantic Journal of Business, 35(2 & 3),* 93-104.

Specialist Bibliography

Bell, J., & Countiss, J. (1993). Professional service throughy sport management internships. *Journal of Physical Education, Recreation and Dance*, *61(1)*, 45-47, 52.

Brassie, P.S. (1989). A student buyer's guide to sport management programs. *Journal of Physical Education, Recreation and Dance. 60(9),* 25-28.

Brassie, P.S. (1989). Guidelines for programs preparing undergraduate and graduate students for careers in sport management. *Journal of Sport Management, 3(2),* 158-164.

Bridges, F.L., & Roquemore, L.L. (1996). *Management for athletic/sport administration: Theory and practice* (2nd ed.). Decatur, GA: ESM Books.

Cambell, K., & Kovar, S.K. (1994). Fitness/exercised science internships: How to ensure success. *Journal of Physical Education, Recreation and Dance*, *65(2),* 69-72.

DeSensi, J., Kelley, D., Blanton, M., & Beitel, P. (1990). Sport management curricular evaluation and needs assessment: A multifaceted approach. *Journal of Sport Management, 4(1),* 31-58.

Lipsey, R.A. (Ed.). (2000). *Sports market place*. Phoenix, AZ: Sportsguide.

Mawson, L.M. (1993). Total quality management: Perspectives for sport management. *Journal of Sport Management, 7(5),* 101-106.

Moss, A. (Ed.). (2000). *The sports business directory*. Bethesda, MD: E. J. Krause & Associates.

Parkhouse, B.L. (1996). *The management of sport: Its foundation and application* (2nd ed). St. Louis, MO: Mosby-Year Book, Inc.

Parks, J.B., & Zanger, B.R. (Eds.). (1990). *Sport & fitness management: Career strategies and profesional content.* Champaign, IL: Human Kinetics Books.

Plunkett, W.R., & Attner, R. (1994). *Introduction to management.* (5th ed.). Belmont, CA: Wadsworth Publishing Company.

Ross, C.M., Jamieson, L.M., & Young, S.J. (1997). *Professional preparation in sports management.* Bloomington, IN: Indiana University Press.

Sawyer, T.H. (1993). Sport management: Where should it be housed? *Journal of Physical Education, Recreation and Dance, 57(8),* 26-27.

Sutton, W.A. (1989). The role of internships in sport management curricula: A model for development. *Journal of Physical Education, Recreation and Dance, 60(7),* 20-24.

Widdon, S. (1990). Graduate dual preparation programs in business and sport management. *Journal of Physical Education, Recreation and Dance, 61(3),* 96-98.

Corporate Model of Sport
Japan's Case

Masaru Ikeda[†]

Introduction

Corporate sport has assumed an important part of Japanese life since modern sports were imported from the West late in the 19th century. Along with rapid economic development after World War II, most Japanese companies have offered sport as an effective measure to facilitate seniority and lifetime employment systems, which have been based on corporate loyalty. Company teams are sponsored and top athletes are hired. These company-sponsored teams and athletes have been contributing to sport in Japanese society and continue to serve as representatives at the Olympic Games and other world-class events. Because of the recent economic recession, however, corporate sport has been struggling to change its role. A large number of companies have been faced with suspension of their sponsored teams and clubs. Increasing emphasis has been placed on promoting workplace health not only by corporations, but also by governments, due to the ageing of the labour force population and the need to reduce the burden of medical care cost.

Sport as A Measure of Labour Management

Company-sponsored sport or corporate sport has played a significant and unique role as the foundation for development of sport in Japan. Modern sports were introduced from the West to Japanese society late in the 19th

Correspondence to: Sasakawa Sports Foundation (SSF), 1-15-16 Toranomon, Minato-ku, Tokyo, 1005-0001, Japan century. Just as it has been reshaped gradually into a Japanese style, Japanese companies have emphasised the value of sport as one of their welfare programmes for employees, especially in the mid-1950s when economic conditions began to improve at a rapid pace. They provided sport facilities, daily exercise break programmes, teams and clubs both at competitive and recreational levels, and special events such as Undo-kai (an athletic festival) for their employees. These services and programmes have been offered as "cradle-to-grave" or lifetime employment benefits that attract and keep good personnel. Corporate sport offered a good opportunity by which the company could channel an employee's energy into a more enthusiastic attitude toward work. It was also expected to create an atmosphere of fellowship and co-operation within the workplace and to build up corporate loyalty.

These paternalistic employment practices of Japanese corporations have been welcomed by their employees who had little opportunity to engage in sport and physical activities after graduation from school. These situations could be seen through some of the statistical data on sport at that time. According to the comprehensive nation-wide survey by the Ministry of Education in 1969, Japan had approximately 150,000 sports facilities at that time. Of the total, about 70% belonged to schools from elementary to the university levels. Only 7% were public facilities provided mainly by local governments, in contrast with 16% provided by corporations for employee use. However, the follow-up survey in 1998 showed a dramatic increase in public sports facilities with 25% of the total 258,000 facilities provided by central, state, or local governments, as compared with 5% for corporate facilities.

Additional data show that Japanese employees still enjoy playing sports with their colleagues at work. According to the National Sport Life Survey conducted by Sasakawa Sports Foundation in 1998, 35% of office and factory workers were affiliated with their company-sponsored sports clubs.

Sport as Public Relations

When referring to corporate sport in Japan, mention must be made of company athletes and teams (Jitsugyo-dan) and their contributions not only to their companies, but also to sport society in Japan.

In accordance with high economic growth and popularity of sports on television since the 1964 Tokyo Olympic Games, Japanese corporations have come to realise the media value of sport in improving their corporate image and promoting sales of products and services. As a result, companies have recruited athletes who have excelled in a sport in high schools and universities. Although they are hired as regular employees, their jobs are not in production or sales, but rather as members of the company team. Companies provide sport facilities and training camps and pay most of the expenses for their athletes and coaches. The term "Company amateurs" is now often used to described Japan's company athletes, just as the former Eastern Bloc countries called these athletes "state amateurs" who received the full support from the state (Ohno et al., 1997). Company amateurs have been among the best in the nation and account for most of Japan's representatives at the Olympics and other international events.

However, due to the collapse of Japan's "bubble economy" since the early 1990s, a large number of companies are now being forced to reduce their employee numbers and adopt alternative measures. The National Bureau of Statistics has reported that the unemployment rate reached 4.8% (3.4 million workers) in March 1999, which was the worst record since World War II, compared with the rate of 1.1% in 1970. Company teams have been discontinued or temporally halted. Company amateurs are often asked to transfer to other company teams or find "patrons". According to the recent survey by *Asahi Shimbun*, one of the leading newspapers, 177 company-sponsored teams have halted or disappeared since 1991, including Nichiban-Kaizuka (a cotton spinning company) women's volleyball team that won a Gold Medal at the Tokyo Olympic Games. Seventy-eight percent of these were scrapped due to a business slump and restructuring of companies.

Sport as Health Promotion

Over the past decades, many Japanese corporations as well as governmental agencies have initiated health and fitness programmes to cope with serious sociomedical problems. One of the major problems Japan is currently faced with is the ageing of its labour force population.

Life expectancy of the Japanese has shown a remarkable improvement. Up to the 1920s, the average life expectancy was only 45 years for both males and females. Presently, it has reached the highest level in the world: 77.16 years for males and 84.01 years for females in 1998. The age structure of the Japanese population changed markedly from the typical pyramid shape with a broad base in the 1930s to the bottle shape in 1980s and to the rectangular shape today. The proportion of the productive age population (15 to 64 years of age) is now approximately 70%, at the highest level among major developed countries. However, the aged population (65 years old and over) is projected to reach 25% in 2025. This estimate demonstrates the extent of the ageing population structure in Japan. The labour force will shift to an ageing population as well. As a result of the increase of the middle aged and older workers in the workplace, Japanese corporations have been paying much attention to the health problems of their employees.

The quality of lifestyle among Japanese workers has changed rapidly and dramatically. Machines and computers now supply the "muscle power" for most daily life activities at home and at the work-site. According to a nation-wide health and fitness survey conducted by the Ministry of Labour in 1982, 50.6% of the Japanese workers described their lifestyles as very inactive and stressful. Inactive and stressful lifestyles, adding to an unhealthy diet, have caused an increase in "lifestyle related disease" such as cancer, heart diseases, hypertension, stroke, osteoporosis and diabetes. The highest rate of death per 100 thousand in 1998 was attributed to cancer (226.6), followed by heart disease (114.2), and cerebrovascular disease (110.0).

As a result of the ageing of the population and the change in lifestyle, the national medical care costs in Japan have been escalating dramatically during the last decade. In 1999, it cost about 30.1 trillion yen which is

7.9% of the national income. Growth in the cost of treatment of older people is particularly great which accounted for 37% of national medical care cost. Currently, every Japanese person spends 238 thousand yen per year.

Along with escalating national medical care expenditures, financial burdens to both Japanese employers and employees have also usurped huge amounts of money. This trend will continue. Employers and employees have been aware of the huge investment in health care, while getting only a modest return for it. Therefore, an increasing number of Japanese corporations have begun offering well organised heath/fitness programmes for employees in order to save the medical care expenditures and to improve productivity. For example, *Asahi Shimbun*, hired full-time fitness directors and instructors. One of their unique programmes is called a "delivery stretching exercise" in which the instructors visit the office not only at the headquarters, but also in several workplaces in Tokyo. Photograph 1 depicts this unique programme.

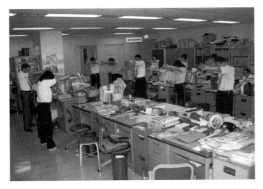

Photo 1: *"Delivery stretch exercise" by Asahi Shimbun*

Nippon Steel Corporation, the largest steel company in Japan, has initiated a comprehensive health/fitness programme after they decided to extend employees' retirement age from fifty-five to sixty years old. Employees from thirty-five to forty-five years old are required to participate at least twice a week in a 12 week supervised fitness class at the company's health promotion centres. In order to analyse the effects of this programme on medical care costs, the company conducted a follow-up survey with the employees who had medical problems such as obesity, diabetes and hypertension. As shown in Table 1, the high adherence group who engaged in vigorous exercise and physical activity regularly for more than one year following participation in the fitness class, reduced medical care costs by almost one half, compared with costs before participating in the programme (Sugahara, 1986).

Exercise Level After Class	Medical Care Cost				
	'81	'82	'83	Average for 3 yrs.	Rate of Reduction*
High Adherence (N = 24)	yen 23,300	yen 21,300	yen 23,500	yen 22,700	% 44.5
Low Adherence (N = 28)	44,800	42,300	43,700	43,600	85.4
Non Exercise (N = 15)	38,600	29,700	41,800	36,700	71.9
Average	35,600	31,800	36,000	34,500	67.6

Effects After Participating in Fitness Class on Medical Care Cost at Nippon Steel Co.

* 100 for 51,000 yen that the average medical cost of the subjects before participating in the fitness class

Table 1: Effects on medical care costs after participating in fitness classes

The Japanese government has also been concerned with corporate fitness programmes as a measure of reducing the national medical care expenditures. The Ministry of Labour proposed the "Total Health Promotion Plan (THP)", which was aimed at health promotion for middle-aged and older workers. In order to develop THP, the Ministry provided two types of subsidies to the companies. The first subsidy, "Aid for Health Check and Health Guidance", was limited to 15 million yen a year per workplace for three years. One-third of expenses (two thirds for companies with less than 300 employees) could be claimed. To receive the subsidy, a complete health, work and lifestyle analysis was conducted and, if necessary, mental health care or nutrition guidance added.

A second subsidy, "Aid for Equipment for Health Check or Exercise", was made to a joint enterprise group (a group of enterprises including a group of workplaces in the same company). A limit of one third of the expense and 20 million yen was made for health analysis and exercise equipment. Corporate incentives to develop health promotion programmes and services at workplaces have been testimony to the government's dedication to employee health.

Conclusion

Corporate sport has played a significant role in promoting sport in Japanese society. However, the country is now facing a substantial crisis due to the economic decline of Japanese corporations. In order to overcome this critical situation, the Japanese Higher Council on Health, Physical Education and Sports proposed to the Ministry of Education, Science, Sports and Culture the "National Proposals for Promoting Health and Sports for All" in 1997. In accordance with this proposal, the Japanese government passed a bill for a soccer lottery "Toto", which raises funds for the development of sport in Japanese society (Ikeda, 1999). It will be introduced in March 2001, and it is expected that 180 billion yen in annual sales well be generated from this lottery. Fifty percent of lottery revenues will be used to pay off lottery winners, 15% will be used for operating costs, and the remaining 35% will be divided equally for the three purposes of promoting sport in communities and at workplaces, developing high-performance sport, and replenishing the national tax coffers. It will be expected that the introduction of "Toto" will facilitate the restructuring of Japanese sport.

References

Ikeda, M. (1999). World trends and strategies for building participation. *ASFAA Newsletter*, Spring, 6-10.

Ministry of Education, Science, Sports and Culture (1998). *Mental and physical health and sports: Japanese government policies in education, science, sports and culture.*

Ministry of Health and Welfare (1999*). Statistical review on national medical treatment expenditures* (in Japanese).

Ohno, A. et al. (1997). *Sports in Japan*. Tokyo: Foreign Press Center.

Sasakawa Sports Foundation (1998). *National Sport Life Survey* (in Japanese. Abstract in English).

Sugahara, K. (1986). Health investment of the Nippon Steel Corporation. *Japanese Journal of Physical Education*. 36,193-199. (in Japanese)

NATION-BUILDING AND THE BUSINESS OF SPORT

The Case of South Africa

Denver Hendricks

Introduction

When South Africa set out upon its course of rebuilding after the unprecedented changes that befell the country following centuries of racial division and discrimination, observers and actors within the country and abroad were of the opinion that the task would not be an easy one. Indeed, the social re-engineering exercise, it was recognised, would provide a laboratory for the world which would put human resilience, ingenuity, tolerance, and other characteristics to the test; the task of undoing the consequences of the apartheid system would be a mammoth one. Indeed, some believed that it would be insurmountable and that it would take extra-ordinary restraint to prevent the situation from deteriorating into violence and anarchy, a scenario that would probably have seen the utter demise of the society, as no single interest group could possibly have prevailed.

Several years have passed since the country embarked on a road of renewal, and it might be opportune at this juncture, to reflect on progress made toward building a new, united nation. In the context of this chapter, the intention, specifically, is to consider whether sport has had any impact on the unfolding social landscape since 1992[1] and particularly so, as that relates to nation building. It is early, by any account, to expect that the situation would have changed so considerably to conclude that the objective of achieving the unified, egalitarian society should have been accomplished.

---

[1] The unification of sport in South Africa preceded the first democratic elections in 1994.

Correspondence to: Prof. Denver Hendricks, Head: Sport and Recreation South Africa, Private Bag X 896, Pretoria 0001, South Africa. E-mail: denver@sport1.pwv.gov.za

Contrarily, there are those who argue that the situation may have deteriorated. They argue, for example, that unemployment is on the increase with more than 504,366 jobs having been shed in the formal sector between 1995 and 1999[2], while crime statistics appear to be worsening. At the other end of the spectrum there are those who would argue that conditions of the majority of people have improved substantially, and that the process of actualising the utopian society is an ongoing, long-term project.

The most telling commentary on the state of change in South Africa, arguably, came from the then Deputy President (and now President) of the country, Thabo Mbeki, who noted that "South Africa is a country of two nations". It may be worthwhile, at this juncture, to consider his statement in more detail, as it is a recurring theme in both his, and the ruling party's, current view of the state of the nation. He commented:

> South Africa is a country of two nations – one white and wealthy, the other black and poor.
>
> The white nation is relatively prosperous, regardless of gender or geographical dispersal. It has ready access to a developed economic, physical, educational, communication and other infrastructure.
>
> This enables it to argue that, except for the persistence of gender discrimination against women, all members of this nation have the possibility to exercise their right to equal opportunity – the development opportunities to which the constitution of 1993 committed our country.
>
> The second and larger nation of South Africa is black and poor, with the worst affected being women in the rural areas, the black rural population in general and the disabled.
>
> This nation lives under conditions of a grossly underdeveloped infrastructure. It has virtually no possibility to exercise what in reality amounts to a theoretical right to equal opportunity.

---

[2] Sunday Times, 7 May 2000, p23, Col 2

> We are not one nation, but two nations....and neither are we becoming one nation. Consequently the objective of national reconciliation is not being realised.

President Mbeki's statement provides a revealing perspective on the state of nation-building in South Africa since 1994, in that it relates unity to features of such an idealised circumstance. He unambiguously refers to access to economic, physical, educational, communication and other infrastructure by all South Africans as cornerstones of nation-building. Aspects such as job security, privacy, a stable family life, appreciation and respect of each other's cultures, religious freedom and tolerance can be added to the list to complete the picture. Access to sport and recreation will certainly form part of the list.

References to the nation-building role of sport in the literature, however, extends well beyond the realm of access to the institution, whether in the form of participation opportunities, or available facilities. It relates, rather, to some mystical potential that sport possesses to secure positive outcomes for the nation as a whole. The effect is usually a consequence of the performance of national or representative teams, or by virtue of the opportunities that it creates directly or vicariously for people to meet or interact and in so doing develop affinities that, ostensibly, translate into national solidarity. Apart from the inherent reification of the assumption – sport is an inanimate concept that cannot possibly dictate the outcomes of human behaviour – it also inadvertently assumes that the outcomes will necessarily be positive. This is a fallacy for sport has also led to conflict, death and other negative consequences.

Sport, instead, is merely a medium that can be exploited by interest groups striving to achieve particular outcomes that further their particular cause. Governments, political parties, and dominant groups may, for example, use sport as a medium to further their own ends.

Of course, observations or interpretations about the potential of, or the actual "role" of sport in society is largely a function of the theoretical disposition from which such analyses are broached. In that regard, needless to say, there are numerous schools of thought. The most popular of these are the functionalist and critical approaches. It might be expedient to reflect on these, albeit superficially at this juncture.

The functionalist approach

In this approach sport is an integrator (Coakley, 1993). This, according to protagonists of this school, is the role that sport plays in nation building. It instils within people the same basic values that promote the union of major parts of the society in mutually supportive and constructive ways. Sport contributes to the fulfilment of the four basic system needs:

- The need for pattern maintenance, i.e. it teaches people common, basic values and norms;
- The need for social integration, i.e. sport creates and strengthens the social relationships that are necessary for people to continue co-operating in constructive ways;
- The need for goal attainment, i.e. the extent to which sport legitimises and reaffirms the important goals in a social system;
- The need for adaptation, i.e. the extent to which participation in sport contributes to preparing people for coping with the challenges of the external, physical and social environments.

Smith (1993) concurs with this position in his commentary on the social integration and socialising role of sport. He argues that sport is especially important, for it integrates various social structures ranging from schools through communities to entire countries. Common interests, loyalties and enthusiasms that protagonists of this school argue are great integrating factors in any culture, and are promoted through sport. Moreover, sports heroes and the identification of the society with them, help satisfy the need for affiliation. An interest in sport, Smith (1993) argues, serves as a catalyst that brings people together on common ground, where their interaction creates a sense of community. In analysing the "role" of soccer in Brazil, for example, Lever (1983) concludes that:

> Sport contributes to national integration by giving people of different social classes, ethnicities, races and religions something to share and use as a basis of their ritual solidarity.

In a nutshell, the above extract epitomises the functionalist approach.

The conflict theory approach

From this perspective, social order results from the fact that some groups of people are able to use their resources to coerce and manipulate others to accept their view of the world as the correct one (Coakley, 1986). In particular, sports promote the interests of those in power by:

- Alienating people;
- The coercion and control of the population by those who possess economic resources and power;
- The development of commercialism;
- The growth of nationalism and militarism;
- The perpetuation of racism and sexism.

Two points are of particular relevance to the South African circumstance in this regard. The first relates to the coercive role of those who posses economic power. Their influence contributes, for example, to sowing division within the ranks of the oppressed. So in South African sport, for example, it is not abnormal to find that members of disadvantaged groups deny or condemn the efforts of those who struggle to actualise the ideals of equality in sport. Individuals from disadvantaged backgrounds who are selected to national teams often criticise the role of campaigners who struggle to ensure representivity of such teams in terms of the racial demographics of the society by insisting on racial quota systems and other such strategies. They prefer to believe and argue that they have been selected on the basis of their inherent talent and hard work, the argument, incidentally, also used by those in control to justify their dominance, rather than as a result of campaigns to ensure representivity.

Secondly, the question of the role of sport in dividing the races (and sexes), and in the perpetuation of racial stereotypes will surface in any consideration of the social dynamics in South African society. In the analysis of sport in society, conflict theorists propose that sport functions to maintain the status quo. The implications for its "role" in South Africa, with regard to racism and sexism is, therefore, obvious. Coakley (1986), quoting Hoch, contends that sport contributes to distorting people's perspectives and encourages self-defeating behaviour. Failure to perform in sports, it is propagated, must be blamed on the individual alone and must be accepted as an indication of personal inadequacy and a need to work harder in the future. At the same time, it distracts workers from becoming involved in political or revolutionary organisations. In other words, sport is an opium for the masses. In South Africa, the masses refer to the black working class. This contributes to the maintenance of the status and privilege of those in power.

In comparison, it would appear that the functionalist approach focuses on the positive consequences of sport in society and, hence, in the nation building process. Conflict theorists, on the other hand tend to be negativistic and critical of the institution of sport generally, and hence of its potential in nation building.

In his evaluation of value of the two theories used for explaining sport in society, Coakley (1986) concludes that both are useful and that one has to be cognisant of the ideas inherent in them. Each of their explanations of the relationship between sport and society alerts us to questions that must be asked and hypotheses that must be tested. In terms of nation-building it is obvious, therefore, that analyses from a functionalist perspective will propagate a positive "role" for sport, epitomised in Lever's (1983) analysis of soccer in Brazil. She concluded that:

> "Soccer brought people together from all over Brazil. It gave them a set of common symbols and a basis for identity and interaction...it was possible to forget their exclusive and tightly defined in-groups and join together with others from a wide variety of different backgrounds."

To illustrate the opposing viewpoint, Coakley (1986) cites Klein's critique of Lever's work that points out that while soccer may have brought people together, there must be doubt about whether that unity had any impact on the political and economic realities of Brazilian life. While it created "emotional unity", it did not help people deal with their differences constructively. In particular, he asks questions about whether:

- Some groups benefit from the "unity" more than others, and
- Whether the unity has any impact on issues apart from sport.

The latter is significant in the South African context to the extent that the lack of unity is probably related more to issues of socio-economic and political discrepancies, rather than the need for emotional concurrence. In the former, the dominant whites have benefited significantly to the extent that the shackles of sports isolation have been broken while the racial composition of national, representative teams have hardly changed.

In the eyes of Thabo Mbeki, there continues to exist two nations in South Africa. The nation-building effort, whatever that may have entailed, has clearly not produced the required outcomes. Moreover, if sport has had any role to play in this regard, that has not materialised either, despite romantic claims to the contrary. It may have created the temporary states of emotional unity referred to above, but has not impacted on economic, physical, educational, communication, health, and other critical aspects of the lives of the majority of the country's people, that have earlier been defined as the foundation upon which nation-building can proceed.

It may be useful to examine the South African landscape more closely at this stage to analyse sport in the context of nation-building. It may also be expedient to explain, albeit very cursorily, an alternative paradigm that will be used in this treatise, to discuss sport in South Africa and, indeed, reflect on its potential or lack thereof, for nation-building.

From this alternative viewpoint, society, contrary to the classical analyses described above, is regarded as a figuration of competing and co-operating interest groups in dynamic interaction with one another. This "figurationalist" approach, was popularised in the work of sociologist Norbert Elias (see Mennel, 1989). Power, he contended, constitutes a central feature of the relationship between groups. The relative access to it by different groups is determined by the extent to which they are able to exert control over, or monopolise access to resources that are not necessarily restricted to those in the economic sphere. The theory of established-outsider relations (Elias & Scotson, 1965) which, in the South African situation can be reduced simplistically to relations between the enfranchised and disenfranchised in the former apartheid regime, is particularly pertinent in this regard.

In Thabo Mbeki's delineation of the two nations in South Africa, the overwhelming white and wealthy nation constitutes the "established", while the majority black and poor constitutes the "outsiders" in this theoretical school. The power of the established is vested in their monopoly of virtually all the (scarce) resources in the society with the exception of political power that was, ostensibly, usurped by the black majority in the country's first democratic elections in 1994. The hesitance to be emphatic in latter regard, relates to the fact that the state machinery is still dominated, in key areas, by officials from the expired, apartheid regime. They are able to effectively stifle transformation and inhibit progress, a situation bolstered by the relative inexperience of the growing black, civil service corps that renders their counter efforts futile. Effectively, therefore, the status quo has remained virtually unchanged since 1994.

The power and privilege of the established is, however, not guaranteed. They have to work very hard to preserve it. Moreover, with the changes that have taken place in South Africa, it is no longer possible to entrench one's dominance or that of a particular group by overtly coercive means, even though vestiges of this still remain. (In latter regard, the forcible eviction of impoverished, black farm workers from their homes by white farm owners, illustrate the point.) The power and privilege of the established has to be secured, rather, by more subtle means. This can be achieved by convincing their own corps as well as the outsiders, of the legitimacy of their status of privilege and power on the basis of their having earned it and, therefore, being deserving of it. At the same time, they have to persuade the outsiders to accept their disqualification from access to "real" power and privilege.

One way of contributing to the achievement of this outcome is through the promotion of the "social habitus" of each of the groups. Social habitus (see Elias & Scotson, 1965) refers to a characterisation of the relative qualities of the established as a "charismatic" group, and the outsiders as "disgraceful". Outsiders, (blacks in South Africa in this case) are characterised as a minority of the worst, in which the despicable traits of a small minority within the group are promoted as being representative of the whole group. In this respect, they are regarded, amongst others, as being dirty, lazy, helpless, unintelligent, incapable, unreliable, feckless and incompetent. The established, on the other hand, are portrayed as a majority of the best with exactly the opposite features to those of the outsiders. These characteristics are generally those positive traits of a minority within the group that is portrayed as being representative of the majority. This notion has to be confirmed consistently and constantly. It is in this regard that sport, in this thesis, is considered to play a significant role. The following examples serve to illustrate the strategy and the point:

- Blacks are significantly underrepresented on national sport teams, ostensibly because they are not sufficiently talented or capable, they do not work hard enough, they are undisciplined, or are just plain lazy;
- The few black members of national teams are not disciplined. Herschelle Gibbs, a black member of the national cricket team, for example, prefers to party late at night while his teammates are resting in preparation for the next day's match as good, disciplined players should be doing. He is accordingly sanctioned for his behaviour. He is particularly fond of vodka (Hayward, 2000). His white counterparts do not exhibit similar irresponsible behaviour.
- The black members of representative teams are cheats. Along with the captain of the national cricket team, two of the three black team members had to be sanctioned for accepting bribes to "fix" a cricket match on an international tour. The white members of the team, some of whom were also suspected of being interested in participating in the scheme, emerged from the scandal with their honour restored.
- A black member of the national cricket team (Herschelle Gibbs again), is portrayed as being "a lot of fun", epitomising the happy-go-lucky and less than serious disposition of the group (blacks) that he purportedly represents.
- Hardly any blacks participate, let alone excel, in aquatic sports. These sports are portrayed as being technically advanced, and blacks are, therefore, incapable of mastering them. In any case, blacks are not particularly fond of water, a perception that reinforces the notion that they are unclean.
- Blacks dominate the sport of football (soccer) in South Africa. This is in order as soccer is regarded as being a working class sport. They are, therefore, expected to be dominant in it. It is not an appropriate sport for the established who do not constitute part of the working

class. Soccer is, therefore, not generally played in schools that are predominantly white.

- A black player in the national rugby team, the Springboks (Breyton Paulse), is noted for scoring "opportunist" tries[3]. The implication is that his effort is generally not part of a well thought out plan. His actions (and, by implication, those of the group that he represents) are, therefore, sporadic and spontaneous, a reflection of similar dispositions in their lifestyles generally.

Many other, similar examples can be cited. Moreover, outstanding performances of outsiders in sport in South Africa are seldom acknowledged outside of the context of that discussed above. This all contributes to painting a picture of the negative social habits of blacks. By the same token, the characterisation of the established (whites) is exactly the opposite. Their performances are characteristic of what is to be expected of a "superior" group. Through these messages even outsiders start to doubt their own capabilities and, hence, the legitimacy of their claims to the power and privilege that remains the monopoly of the established.

The role of the media in promoting the relative habits of each of the groups and, hence, in entrenching notions of who should be eligible for power and privilege is paramount.   An exposition of their role in this regard, unfortunately, falls beyond the scope of this chapter.

In essence, therefore, this brief insight into the contribution of sport to the social order in South Africa, is one of preserving the status quo and hence division and inequality within society, rather than that of building one nation. The famous victory of the national rugby team, the Springboks, in the 1995 Rugby World Cup in Johannesburg, South Africa when the then President Nelson Mandela donned the Captain's jersey is seen as having been a lost opportunity when the rugby authorities ostensibly failed to capitalise on the goodwill of the groups that emerged as a result of it. The exposition above, effectively dispels the notion that anything concrete could have come of this as sport could hardly have impacted on any of the aspects identified by President Thabo Mbeki as being responsible for creating the two, divided nations in South Africa. At best it could only create

---

[3] A try (pl. tries) is the equivalent of a goal in the game of rugby.

the temporary "emotional high" described earlier. Unfortunately, that high dissipates soon after the excitement of the stadium has died down and people return to their lives of relative unequal privilege and power in society. The longer term effects, rather, could be exactly the opposite, namely that of entrenching the divisions that prevail, as explained above.

This is not to say that sport can never be used as a medium in nation-building. The prerequisite for this, however, would be the elimination of the divisive elements that hamper unity in the nation, as identified by Thabo Mbeki. The nation will first have to become more homogenous with regard to the material conditions of the various groups. Unfortunately, the prevailing discrepancies will not be eradicated overnight.

References

Coakley, J. (1993). Sport in Society: An Inspiration or an Opiate? In Eitzen, D.S. (Ed.) *Sport in Contemporary Society: An Anthology (4th Edition)*. New York: St. Martin's Press.

Coakley, J. (1986). *Sport in Society: Issues and Controversies, (3rd Edition)*. St Louis: Times Mirror/Mosby.

Hayward, N. (Ed). (2000). Herschelle Gibbs. *SA Cricket Action*, 5.7, 64.

Lever, J. (1983). *Soccer Madness.* Chicago: University of Chicago Press.

Mennel , S. (1989). *Norbert Elias: Civilization and the Human Self-Image*. Basil Blackwell.

Elias, N. & Scotson, J. (1965). *The Established and the Outsiders: A Sociological Enquiry into Community Problems*. Frank Cass.

Smith, G.J. (1993). The Noble Sports Fan. In Eitzen, D.S. *Sport in Contemporary Society: An Anthology (4th Edition)*. New York: St. Martin's Press.

SPORT AND TOURISM

Capitalising on the Linkage

Laurence Chalip

Introduction

In a forecast of business sector growth during the 21st century, Molitor (2000) predicted that sport and tourism would each rank among the industries that would account for the dominant share of gross domestic product (GDP) during the 21st century – particularly in industrialised countries. Molitor observed that tourism had already become the third largest retail industry in the United States, and cited figures showing that sport and travel were among the fastest growing free time activities of Americans. In 1996, the World Travel and Tourism Council (WTTC) estimated that tourism accounted for 10.7% of world economic output. The WTTC also noted that tourism was growing faster than the world economy as a whole, and projected that tourism would account for 11.5% of world economic output by 2006.

Meanwhile, estimates of sport's impact on the economies of Australia (Ernst & Young, Inc. & Tasman Asia Pacific, 1998) and the United States (Meek, 1997; Sandomir, 1988) indicate that by the end of the 20th century, sport was contributing approximately 1% to GDP, ranking it among those countries' 25 largest industries. An Australian national export strategy study during the same period found that export earnings from sport could be tripled over a ten year period, and that tourism generated through sport would be a pivotal driver of that growth (Price Waterhouse, Urwick &

Correspondence to: Dr. Laurence Chalip, School of Marketing and Management, Griffith University, PMB 50 Gold Coast Mail Centre, Queensland 9726, Australia
Tel +61 7 5594 8722; Fax +61 7 5594 8085; E-mail: L.Chalip@mailbox.gu.edu.au

Maxwell and Druce International, 1996). Recent European work documented the use of sport as a core element of the marketing mix for five of Europe's largest cities (van den Berg, Braun, & Otgaar, 2000). Sport played a significant role in the economic growth of Barcelona, Helsinki, Manchester, Rotterdam, and Turin – largely as a result of the ways that sport helped to make the cities appealing places to visit.

The Convergence of Sport and Tourism

Findings like those cited above have highlighted the emerging convergence of sport and tourism. The convergence has been dubbed, "sport tourism" (cf. Delpy, 1998; Gibson, 1998). Although sport tourism has been defined differently by different authors, the varied definitions have recently been synthesised by Standeven and De Knop (1999), who describe it as, "All forms of active and passive involvement in sporting activity, participated in casually or in an organised way for non-commercial or business/commercial reasons, that necessitate travel away from home and work locality" (p. 12).

In point of fact, the convergence of sport and tourism is neither new nor unique to European cultures. Travel to watch or participate in sport has been noted in non-European cultures (Blanchard, 1995), and has been documented for ancient Greece (Golden, 1998), Rome (Futrell, 1997; Humphrey, 1986), and medieval Europe (Carter, 1981). By the late 19th century, sport had found its way into the marketing mix of tourist resorts (Gibson, 1998).

What is new is the institutionalisation of the linkage between sport and tourism. Historically, sport and tourism have been treated as separate realms of endeavour. Sport developed an array of governance institutions specifically concerned with sport (Thoma & Chalip, 1996), while the governance of tourism developed separately. As a consequence, although recent years have seen a substantial increase in sport tourism activity, there has been little liaison between the agencies traditionally responsible for sport and those that are responsible for tourism (Standeven & De Knop, 1999; Weed & Bull, 1997). Consequently, policies intended to promote one have rarely been made to synergise with policies intended to promote the other.

In some countries, policymakers have endeavoured to overcome the disconnect between policymaking for sport and policymaking for tourism by developing institutions to focus on the linkage. For example, between 1985 and the mid-1990s, the Australian states of Queensland, Victoria, and Western Australia established events corporations whose purpose is to attract (and sometimes to subsidise) special events. Large sport events have been the primary target of those units (Chalip & Mules, 1997). During the same period in the United States, local sports commissions were established in over 100 municipalities. In nearly every instance, the commissions work to attract sport events to their region, but in some cases the commission's mandate is broader, including development of facilities, and attraction of visitors to use those facilities <http://www.sportscommisions.org>.

The creation of a new authority with a specific focus on sport tourism has merely added another unit to the policymaking bureaucracy. As a result, new complexities are sometimes created without generating the desired synergies (cf. Chalip & Mules, 1997). In order to prevent that, some governments have sought to build sport tourism as a niche focus of the existing tourism authority. Thus, in 1996 the Canadian Tourism Commission formulated the Canadian Sports Tourism Initiative to foster coordinated development of sport tourism at community level <http://www.canadatourism.com>, and in 2000 the British Tourism Authority launched a sport tourism marketing strategy (Tippey, 2000). In Australia, the Australian Capital Territory and the state of New South Wales have events units within their respective tourism departments.

These initiatives have been generated by governments as they attempt to obtain a net economic gain by fostering the linkage between sport and tourism. As the examples indicate, the impetus has been located differently in different countries. In the United Kingdom, it has been national; in Australia, it has been regional (state-based); in the United States, it has been local. These initiatives represent the initial stages of institutionalisation. Over time, we can expect to see some institutionalisation at all three levels of government, as policy rationalisation and implementation will require coordination across the three levels (cf. Chalip & Mules, 1997). Indeed, this need is explicitly noted in the Canadian initiative.

The Structure of Sport Tourism

The institutionalisation of sport tourism, as represented by the policies described above, has focused primarily on fostering sport events. The objective has been to build a positive image for destinations, as well as to attract tourists during the event itself (Getz, 1998). The underlying rationale has been to create an economic boost by building tourist numbers, thereby obtaining a higher aggregate volume of tourist spending.

Although sport events often do stimulate sufficient visitor spending to engender a positive net economic impact (Mules & Faulkner, 1996), a singular focus on sport events as a tourism development strategy can be counter-productive. Indianapolis serves as a case in point. That city invested heavily to attract and host national and international sport events. An independent evaluation of the strategy found no significant gain to the local economy as a result of the investment (Rosentraub, Swindell, Przybylski, & Mullins, 1994). Similarly, a study of nine metropolitan areas of the United States that built new stadiums in order to enable sporting events found that public investment in a stadium failed to contribute to economic development in every case but one (Baade & Dye, 1990). Indeed, when the associated opportunity costs and inequitable distribution of benefits are considered, public investments to obtain and host sport events are of questionable value (Mules, 1998).

The primary limitation of sport tourism policies that focus on events is that the synergies events can have with other forms of sport tourism are then excluded. Gibson (1998) identified three types of sport tourism: tourism to spectate at sport events, tourism to participate in sport, and tourism to visit sport attractions (such as sport museums, halls of fame, or famous facilities). Each of these forms of tourism is potentially supportive of the others. Thus, the same facilities that host events may be used at other times for other forms of participation. For example, facilities that hosted spectators at the 1982 Commonwealth Games in Brisbane, though still used for major events, are also used for sport training camps. Similarly, facilities that are famous for hosting events may also become tourist attractions in themselves. For example, the Olympic Stadium in Barcelona (which is currently home to the soccer club Español) is featured on the route of Barcelona's Bus Turistic. Further, sport facilities may become venues for sport nostalgia even when their primary role is to provide an opportunity to participate in a sport. The golf course at St. Andrews in Scotland is one example.

These examples illustrate a vital point. Sport tourism is not synonymous with sport event tourism. Rather, sport tourism is multi-faceted. Each element of sport tourism – spectating at an event, participating in sport, or engaging in sport nostalgia – can be facilitated by the others. The challenge, then, is to identify ways to create and synergise a destination's mix of sport tourism opportunities.

Sport Tourism and the Destination's Marketing Mix

When planning and marketing a sport tourism mix, it is useful to distinguish two forms of sport tourism – tourism for which sport is the primary objective, and tourism during which sport is an incidental component. For example, Crompton (1995) found that although 57% of tourists attending a particular event had come specifically for the event (i.e., the event was their primary objective), 43% of tourists at the same event had not planned their trip to attend the event (i.e., the event was an incidental component of their tourism activity). The distinction is important because the product mix and associated marketing communications will differ as a function of whether sport is a primary objective or an incidental component of the tourist's visit to a destination.

In order to grasp the practical utility of the distinction, it is useful to consider the ways in which consumers choose a travel destination. When sport is an incidental component of the desired tourism experience, the destination's attractiveness to the consumer will be determined by the presence of relevant sport opportunities *plus the other activities and attractions that the destination can offer* (Dellaert, Borgers, & Timmermans, 1995; Hu & Ritchie, 1993; Woodside & Lysonski, 1989). In other words, sport-related opportunities at the destination may enhance the attractiveness of the destination, but other elements of the destination's product mix (e.g., sight-seeing opportunities, nightlife, entertainment, amenities, weather, etc.) will play a critical role in determining whether or not the destination becomes part of the tourist's itinerary. Consequently, marketing communications promoting the destination to tourists for whom sport is desirable but incidental should emphasise the range of activities and attractions that are available (Gartner & Hunt, 1987). Any sport-related opportunity should feature only as one of a number of activities and attractions that the destination has to offer.

On the other hand, some tourists will choose a destination specifically for the sport-related opportunities that it provides (Getz, 1998; Nogawa, Yamaguchi, & Hagi, 1996; Richards, 1996). In these instances, other activities and attractions at the destination are important to the degree that they complement or support the sport experience (Green & Chalip, 1998). When a sport opportunity is the tourist's primary objective, it will be the fundamental basis for destination choice, and other aspects of the destination will be evaluated primarily in terms of their capacity to complement or enhance the sport experience. Marketing communications promoting the destination to these tourists should feature the relevant sport opportunities. Other aspects of the destination should be presented minimally and in terms of the quality they can add to the sport experience (Goosens, 2000).

Leveraging Sport Tourism

A great deal of the research about sport tourism has focused on its economic impact (Crompton, 1995; Mules & Faulkner, 1996). As the discussion so far demonstrates, however, the impact of any particular sport tourism activity depends substantially on the way that it is combined with other elements of the destination's product mix, and the way it is then promoted. The issue is not so much one of impact as it is one of leverage – that is, finding means to obtain the best possible tourism return from the sport investment.

Two tactics can maximise the revenue generated from a tourist: (1) increase the amount that the tourist spends per day, and (2) lengthen the tourist's stay at the destination, thereby requiring more expenditure (cf. Frechtling, 1987). From a sport tourism perspective, the key to achieving those aims is to bundle each sport activity with other consumption opportunities that will be attractive to the sport tourist. For example, Green and Chalip (1998) found that participants in a women's football tournament particularly enjoyed socialising with other participants, and were willing to invest in food, drink, and extended stays at the destination in order to maximise the opportunity. Similarly, tourists to Barcelona who visit Barça (the city's pre-eminent soccer club) are encouraged to visit the soccer museum that the club has established on its premises. In addition to generating revenue from an admission fee, the visit encourages spending by providing opportunities to purchase memorabilia and souvenirs. The club also features a large sporting goods store where visitors can purchase clothing and sports equipment.

Tourists who watch sport, participate in sport, or visit a sport attraction are demonstrating a particular sporting interest. Interest profiling is a well established component of psychographic market segmentation (Plummer, 1974). Recent work suggests that sport interests are, at least sometimes, associated with distinctive patterns of consumption (Green & Chalip, 1998; Holt, 1995; Schouten & McAlexander, 1995; Wheaton, 2000; Yoder, 1997). Yet we know very little about how the sport interests of tourists are related to one another; nor do we know the ways that tourists' sport interests are related to preferences for particular (non-sport) goods or services. Specification of these relationships would enhance the leveraging of sport tourism by enabling it to be bundled more effectively with other consumption opportunities.

This potential for leveraging a destination's sport tourism elements suggests the value of a portfolio-based approach to sport tourism development (cf. Khurana & Rosenthal, 1997). Accordingly, a destination would catalogue its available and potential sport tourism offerings. It would then identify points of synergy among them, and would locate means to link each to other elements of the destination's product mix. The specific mix of sport tourism elements to be maintained, enhanced, or developed would be chosen (in conjunction with non-sport elements of the product mix) to optimise the aggregate impact on the destination's share of the tourism market.

Although portfolio-based approaches have not been described in the literature for sport tourism in general, portfolio approaches have been advocated for a destination's choice of sport events. Two bases for event portfolio selection have been noted. First, events can be used to attract visitors during periods of the year that would otherwise obtain minimal visitation (Getz, 1997). In other words, sport events are particularly useful when they will bring visitors during times of the year when tourism levels would otherwise be relatively low. In this way, sport event tourists can fill unused tourism capacity.

The second basis for selection of event portfolios derives from the observation that sport events differ in terms of the interest and demographic profiles of their respective audiences or participants. Consequently, it has been suggested that an optimal mix of events will extend the reach and frequency of event-based messages to target market segments (Schreiber & Lenson, 1994). It is argued that by offering an appropriately varied mix of events, the destination can profile itself to varied market segments throughout the year.

This latter example demonstrates that leveraging is not merely a matter of stimulating visitor spending. Sport can also be used to enhance tourist awareness and interest in the destination. This insight formed the basis of the Australian Tourist Commission's strategy for leveraging the Sydney Olympics (Chalip, 2000). The media focus on Australia in the build-up to the Olympic Games (and during the event itself) was used to add depth and breadth to Australia's position in international tourism markets. Media were assisted to find and to research stories about Australia. Partnerships were formed with media and with event sponsors to project Australian images into international markets.

Nurturing the Links between Sport and Tourism

The foregoing discussion demonstrates the utility of developing and marketing sport tourism in terms of the value that it adds to the destination's overall mix of tourism products and services. This would seem to recommend placing responsibility for sport tourism with whichever agency or department is responsible for tourism planning and promotion. However, that solution does not overcome the historic divide between the governance of sport and the management of tourism (Weed & Bull, 1997). Key elements of sport tourism infrastructure remain the responsibility of sport organisations. Sport clubs, sport officials, sport competitions, sport leagues, and many facilities are administered through sport organisations that are concerned minimally (if at all) with tourism. In order for sport tourism policies and programs to be realised, tourism organisations need to develop effective partnerships with sport organisations.

The formation of partnerships takes on added salience when one considers the legitimations for policy initiatives designed to foster sport tourism. In each instance, the motivating rational has been the economic benefits that sport tourism has been expected to bring to a destination. Yet the agencies responsible for local, regional, and national economic development have rarely been included as partners in the formulation or implementation of sport tourism policies. If sport tourism is to be nurtured in a manner consistent with its potential to contribute to economic development, then agencies responsible for cultivating economic growth need to be included in the partnership. Sport tourism will be built most effectively through partnerships that blend tourism, sport, and economic development.

References and Bibliography

Specialist Readings

Baade, R., & Dye, R. (1990). The impact of stadiums and professional sports on metropolitan area development. *Growth and Change, 21*, 1-13.

Blanchard, K. (1995). *The anthropology of sport*. Westport, CT: Bergin & Garvey.

Carter, J.M. (1981). *Ludi medi aevi: Studies in the history of medieval sport*. Manhattan, KS: Kansas State University Press.

Chalip, L. (2000). An interview with Maggie White, Business Manager Olympic Games for the Australian Tourist Commission. *International Journal of Sports Marketing & Sponsorship, 2*, 187-197.

Chalip, L., & Mules, T. (1997, Spring). How sport affects the state of the economy. *Running Sport*, 10-17.

Crompton, J.L. (1995). Economic analysis of sport facilities and events: Eleven sources of misapplication. *Journal of Sport Management, 9*, 14-35.

Dellaert, B., Borgers, A., & Timmermans, H. (1995). A day in the city: Using conjoint choice experiments to model urban tourists' choice of activity packages. *Tourism Management, 16*, 347-353.

Ernst & Young, Inc., & Tasman Asia Pacific (1998). *The economic impact study of sport*. Canberra: Confederation of Australian Sport.

Frechtling, D.C. (1987). Assessing the impacts of travel and tourism: Measuring economic benefits. In J.R.B. Ritchie & C. Goeldner (Eds.), *Travel, tourism, and hospitality research* (pp. 325-331). New York: Wiley.

Futrell, A. (1997). *Blood in the arena: The spectacle of Roman power*. Austin: University of Texas Press.

Gartner, W.C., & Hunt, J.D. (1987). An analysis of state image change over a twelve-year period. *Journal of Travel Research, 26(2)*, 15-19.

Golden, M. (1998). *Sport and society in ancient Greece*. New York: Cambridge University Press.

Goosens, C. (2000). Tourism information and pleasure motivation. *Annals of Tourism Research, 27,* 301-321.

Green, B.C., & Chalip, L. (1998). Sport tourism as the celebration of subculture. *Annals of Tourism Research, 25,* 275-291.

Holt, D.B. (1995). How consumers consume: A typology of consumption practices. *Journal of Consumer Research, 22,* 1-16.

Hu, Y., & Ritchie, J.R.B. (1993). Measuring destination attractiveness: A contextual approach. *Journal of Travel Research, 32(2),* 25-34.

Humphrey, J.H. (1986). *Roman circuses: Arenas for chariot racing.* Berkeley: University of California Press.

Khurana, A., & Rosenthal, S.R. (1997). Integrating the fuzzy front end of new product development. *Sloan Management Review, 38(2),* 103-120.

Meek, A. (1997). An estimate of the size and supported economic activity of the sports industry in the United States. *Sport Marketing Quarterly, 6(4),* 15-21.

Molitor, G.T.T. (2000). Five economic activities likely to dominate the new millennium: The leisure era. *Technological Forecasting and Social Change, 65,* 239-249.

Mules, T. (1998). Taxpayer subsidies for major sporting events. *Sport Management Review, 1,* 25-43.

Mules, T., & Faulkner, B. (1996). An economic perspective on special events. *Tourism Economics, 2,* 314-329.

Nogawa, H., Yamaguchi, Y., & Hagi, Y. (1996). An empirical research study on Japanese sport tourism in sport-for-all events: Case studies of a single-night event and a multiple-night event. *Journal of Travel Research, 35(2),* 46-54.

Plummer, J.T. (1974). The concept of life style segmentation. *Journal of Marketing, 38,* 33-37.

Price Waterhouse, Urwick & Maxwell and Druce International (1996). *Expanding Australia's sporting and recreational links with Asia.* Canberra: Australian Government Publishing Service.

Richards, G. (1996). Skilled consumption and UK ski holidays. *Tourism Management, 17,* 25-34.

Rosentraub, M.S., Swindell, D., Przybylski, M., & Mullins, D.R. (1994). Sport and downtown development strategy: If you build it, will jobs come? *Journal of Urban Affairs, 16,* 221-239.

Sandomir, R. (1988, March 28). The $50 billion sport industry. *Sports Inc.,* 20-23.

Schouten, J.W., & McAlexander, J.H. (1995). Subcultures of consumption: An ethnography of the new bikers. *Journal of Consumer Research, 22,* 43-61.

Tippey, B. (Ed.). (2000, July). *Sports tourism news* [whole issue].

van den Berg, L., Braun, E., & Otgaar, A.H.J. (2000). *Sports and city marketing in European cities.* Rotterdam: euricur.

Weed, M.E., & Bull, C.J. (1997). Integrating sport and tourism: A review of regional policies in England. *Progress in Tourism and Hospitality Research, 3,* 129-148.

Wheaton, B. (2000). "Just do it": Consumption, commitment, and identity in the windsurfing subculture. *Sociology of Sport Journal, 17,* 254-274.

Woodside, A.G., & Lysonski, S. (1989). A general model of traveller destination choice. *Journal of Travel Research, 27(4),* 8-14.

World Travel and Tourism Council (1996). *Travel & tourism's economic impact: 1996/2006.* London: Author.

Yoder, D.G. (1997). A model for commodity intensive serious leisure. *Journal of Leisure Research, 29,* 407-429.

Non-specialist Readings about Sport Tourism

Delpy, L. (1998). An overview of sport tourism: Building towards a dimensional framework. *Journal of Vacation Marketing, 4,* 23-38.

Getz, D. (1998). Trends, strategies, and issues in sport-event tourism. *Sport Marketing Quarterly, 7(2),* 8-13.

Gibson, H. (1998). Sport tourism: A critical analysis of research. *Sport Management Review, 1,* 45-76.

Standeven, J., & De Knop, P. (1999). *Sport tourism.* Champaign, IL: Human Kinetics.

Related Non-specialist Readings

Getz, D. (1997). *Event management and event tourism.* New York: Cognizant Communication.

Schreiber, A., & Lenson, B. (1994). *Lifestyle and event marketing: Building the new customer partnership.* New York: McGraw-Hill.

Thoma, J., & Chalip, L. (1996). *Sport governance in the global community.* Morgantown, WV: F.I.T.

EVENT MANAGEMENT

Lessons for Design and Implementation

B. Christine Green

Introduction

Events play a central role in the production of sport. From weekly community swimming carnivals to broadcasts of the Olympic Games, sporting events touch the lives of people the world over. Event management, then, affects the ways in which people experience sport, either as a participant or as a spectator. While the most visible role of event managers is the production of the competition itself, the purpose of most events goes well beyond the mere staging of a competition among teams or athletes. For many events, the competition, while necessary, is a means to meet any number of less obvious objectives. These objectives focus on one or more of the following: (1) revenue generation, (2) marketing communications, (3) community building, and/or (4) relationship building. Each of these objectives has implications for the design and management of an event.

This chapter begins with a brief history of the development of sport events and a discussion of event types and characteristics. Principles of effective event management are identified, largely based on the application of general management principles in standard functional areas. Unique issues facing event managers are examined and implications for the design and implementation of events are noted. The chapter closes with a discussion of future directions for event management.

Correspondence to: Dr. B. Christine Green, Senior Lecturer, School of Marketing & Management, Griffith University, PMB 50 Gold Coast Mail Centre, Queensland 9726, Australia. Tel. +617 5594 8644, Fax +617 5594 8085; E-mail: c.green@mailbox.gu.edu.au

Historical Development

Sporting events have existed since ancient times (Guttmann, 1986). In fact, the largest event on the modern sporting calendar – the Olympic Games – claims its heritage from ancient Greek athletic contests occurring as early as the eighth century B.C. Similarly, Roman gladiatorial games and chariot races provide evidence of large scale events moving into the fourth century A.D. The event tradition continued through the Middle Ages with medieval knights competing in tournaments that also served as entertainment for feudal society. Throughout history, events continued to be staged wherever participants gathered to compete. It was not until the 1800s, however, that event management took on a more professional focus (Gladden, McDonald, & Barr, 1998).

Barnstorming tours and the emergence of sport organisations such as the Football Association (in England in 1863) and the Amateur Athletic Union in the United States began the bureaucratisation of sport. The development of leagues followed soon after. Arguably, the commercial focus of the leagues led to a more business-like approach to managing sport contests.

Growth in sport participation and sport spectation, both prompted by and supported with increasing television coverage of sport events, precipitated a new era in event management. The emergence of organisations whose sole business was event management speaks to the increasing centrality and profitability of events in the sport business landscape. IMG (International Management Group), an early entrant into the field, began developing and managing events as a strategy to expand the company's control over events in which IMG clients competed (Gladden et al., 1998). IMG and competitors Horst Dassler of Adidas and Patrick Nally of the West Nally Group once controlled nearly every major sport event in the world (McMullen, 1988). Their commercial control was predominately the result of control over players and sponsorship.

The new emphasis on sponsorship and events was a significant factor in the growth of the events industry. As the cost to sponsor events increased, so did the responsibility to produce professionally managed competitions that were accountable to sponsors' objectives. As events became big business, the quantity, variety and impact of sporting events exploded. Consequently, new stakeholder groups became interested in the use of events to meet their own objectives.

City marketers now use events to shape the image of their city, stimulate urban development, and stimulate their economy (van den Berg, Braun, & Otgaar, 2000). Tourism marketers use events to position their destination, reach specific target markets, and fill off-season capacity (Getz, 1998). Governments use events to build community spirit, and to provide jobs and/or training opportunities (McDonnell, Allen, & O'Toole, 1999). Politicians use events to appeal to constituents and garner funding for projects and infrastructure such as new or improved sport facilities (Whitson & Macintosh, 1996). Sponsors use events to increase brand awareness, reach sought after target markets, launch new products, and entertain clients (Schreiber & Lenson, 1994). Sport and recreation organisations use events to provide competitive opportunities, to raise funds, and to promote their sport (Goldfine & Schleppi, 1997). Each of these objectives has implications (albeit, sometimes conflicting implications) for the design and implementation of an event. Very few of these objectives can be met by merely providing a well-run sport competition. Rather, event managers must be willing and able to provide an event product that is not limited to the competition. This requires the incorporation of a range of ancillary activities.

Types of Events

Special events are often categorised by their size and the scale of their impact. McDonnell et al. (1999) use size and impact to classify special events as either:
1. mega-events, such as the Olympic Games or FIFA World Cup,
2. hallmark events, such the Tour de France or Indianapolis 500,
3. major events, such as the Rugby World Cup or America's Cup Race,
4. local events, such as State Masters' Games or a local softball tournament.

From a tourism perspective, mega-events have been defined as:
> "...events which are expressly targeted at the international tourism market and may be suitably described as 'mega' by virtue of their size in terms of attendance, target market, level

of public financial involvement, political effects, extent of television coverage, construction of facilities, and the impact on economic and social fabric of the host community."
(Hall, 1992, p. 5)

Hallmark events are major events that have become uniquely paired with a particular place so that they increase interest in and bestow status on a particular city or place. Major events, then, can be defined as those events which can, by their scale or profile with the media, provide significant economic benefits, media coverage, or visitor numbers (McDonnell et al., 1999). Events not meeting these criteria would be considered local events.

The preceding event typology is somewhat useful to event planners, but does not adequately differentiate sport events from one another. In addition to the categories listed above, four added dimensions can be identified. First, sport events are generally developed with either a spectator or a participant focus. This distinction has immediate implications for facility selection, marketing strategies, and event logistics. Second, the competitive focus of events may vary. Producing a World Cup swim meet would be an altogether different managerial challenge than putting on the local swim club's championship. Third, events can cater for either a single sport or can host multiple sports within the event. Multi-sport events tend to have co-ordination challenges that rarely occur with single sport events. Fourth, an event may be held in a single day or may occur over several days or even weeks. These four dimensions highlight core differences among sport events and facilitate very different objectives. Each dimension is independent of the others and any or all may operate within a single event category (i.e., mega-event, hallmark event, major event, local event). Each also impacts on the design and planning of the event.

Event Planning and Design

Sport and recreation managers have been running competitions for centuries. Consequently, we know a great deal about tournament formats, seeding, scheduling, and administering athletic contests (e.g., American Sport Education Program, 1996; Gunsten, 1978). Basic management functions are now routinely applied in the provision of sport events. Still, managing a sport event is not the same as managing a sport organisation.

To manage an event is to manage a temporary organisation. The temporary nature of the organisation will alter the ways in which functional areas operate.

Event planning occurs on two levels:
1. Organisers should develop a strategic plan for the event. Strategic event planning entails establishing a vision and mission for the event, formulating objectives, performing environmental scanning, and developing the strategies and tactics that enable the organisation to meet its objectives (McDonnell et al., 1999). Each stand-alone event would have its own strategic plan, which would mesh with the mission and objectives of the host organisation.
2. Operational plans are developed to specify the steps needed to implement specific event strategies. Operational plans may be re-used or shared by events.

For events, strategic planning may take on a dual role, at least for major events. First, strategic planning would inform an organisation's bid to host an event. Specific operational plans would be developed for bidding. The purpose of bid planning is to position the organisation as a viable and desirable event host. Bid documents are usually concerned with meeting the objectives of the event owner. The objectives of the host organisation are addressed in the strategic planning for the event itself. Effective event management most often occurs when the goals and objectives of the event owner and event host are aligned.

Due to the temporary nature of the event organisation, event planning is often treated as a project management problem. Like strategic planning, projects begin with clear objectives and a team of people or human resources. It is the fixed time scale, however, that sets project management apart from strategic planning. An event must be delivered on a certain date at a specific time. Project management tools assist event managers to breakdown and schedule tasks, assign resources, and monitor the progress of all components of the event plan (see Reiss, 1995 for a discussion of project management).

Project management techniques assist event managers to assign and monitor resources, not the least of which are human resources. As one would expect in temporary organisations, staffing can prove quite challenging for event managers. Three related issues underscore this challenge: (1) duration of appointments, (2) growth in workforce needs, and (3) staff commitment to the organisation. Even annual events find it difficult to maintain a consistent workforce from month to month. The nature of a project such as a sporting event is such that a small management team is hired to begin the project. As the planning progresses and workloads expand, so does the workforce. Staffing peaks during the event and contracts rapidly thereafter. The result is a small number of long-term appointments and a large number of short-term appointments. Typically, these are supplemented by a mass of casual and/or volunteer workers during the event itself. Short contract periods and increasing numbers of positions to fill can make it difficult to attract qualified applicants. The law of supply and demand suggests that increased supply of jobs will ultimately result in a lower quality workforce. This is compounded by the temporary nature of the staff positions. It would be expected that people with the best qualifications would already have full time employment. Why then, would they leave a regular job for temporary employment? Further, event employees are often asked to work long hours in the lead-up to and during the event. This requires a committed workforce. What is it, then, that keeps event workers committed and focused on the job at hand, knowing that they will be out of work in a matter of days?

Some of the answers may be found in the work on event volunteers. Volunteers, by definition receive no remuneration for their work. What then, motivates them to become an event volunteer? Although individual motives vary, volunteers report significant benefits from their experience (Cuskelly, McIntyre, & Boag, 1998; Farrell, Johnston, & Twynam, 1998; Green & Chalip, 1998a). Typical benefits identified by volunteers include: earning rewards and recognition, learning new skills, meeting new people, helping others, enhancing their status, and experiencing thrills and excitement. With a few exceptions, these benefits are outside our usual human resource management frameworks. In the case of sport, generally, and sport events in particular, volunteering is often framed as a leisure experience rather than as an unpaid work role. Consequently, participation in the event and therefore the sport's subculture is a powerful motivator for many volunteers. The question remains, then, can we design events that satisfy workers' (both paid and unpaid) desire to be a part of the subculture of the sport and the sport event? Further, which elements assist workers to feel connected, and thereby committed to the event?

The need to attract and retain temporary workers such as volunteers, ostensibly a human resource function, has recently been discussed as a marketing task (Green & Chalip, 1998a). From this viewpoint, staff can be seen as one of a variety of client groups that marketing efforts are directed toward. Other client groups or target markets depend on the objectives of the event. Some of the more obvious marketing targets include participants, spectators, sponsors, and media. Marketing efforts directed at these target markets are essentially concerned to create interest in the event that will translate into financial success (e.g., more entries, higher gate receipts, more sponsorship funds, increased rights fees, etc.).

Marketing efforts directed toward participants and spectators share a common focus – each is based on increasing interest in the event experience for its own sake. There has been a great deal of research investigating the consumer behaviour of sport fans and participants. Fans have been found to attend sport events for the social opportunities that occur (Melnick, 1993), because of their attachment to the game (Kahle, Kambara, & Rose, 1996), and in response to their identification with the team (Madrigal, 1995). These attendance motives are fairly stable across studies. Interestingly, these studies examine fan motives at regularly occurring sport events – that is, league games.

Attendance at special events, which seem to have an attraction beyond that of any particular team or sport, is less well understood. Notably, attendance at multi-sport events such as the Commonwealth, Asian, and Pan American Games has rarely been studied. Some attention is given to television viewership of events, particularly the Olympic Games, but viewing motives have been shown to differ markedly from motives to attend an event. One study, in fact, found that people who watched major professional sport events on television were less likely to travel to attend an Olympic Games (Chalip, Green, & Vander Velden, 1998). Chalip (1992) provides a rare discussion of the use of event attractors – specifically, elements of multiple narratives, embedded genres, and layered symbols – to market sport.

Motivation to participate in sport has been well studied (Biddle, 1995; Scanlan & Simons, 1992; Wankel, 1993). More than one hundred motives have been identified by sport participants, but most can be categorised as either social, mastery/competence, fitness, affiliation, achievement, recognition, emotional release, or enjoyment. Still, sport programmers have been slow to design programs that can deliver a sufficiently wide array of desired benefits. Marketers, too, have been slow to capitalise on the extensive volume of research identifying sport participation motives. The notable exception is Brooks' (1998) formulation of a theory linking personal identity to sport participation.

While event marketers can be informed by the literature on sport participation motivation, sport participation per se should not be confused with participation in a sport event. Although participation motivation for events has not been well studied, there has been some research that examines the motives of event participants. Tanabe, Green, and Chalip (1998) studied entrants in different races (marathon, half marathon, 10K run, and 10K walk) at the Gold Coast Marathon. They found that although the motives of entrants did not differ as a function of the race they entered, their involvement and commitment to running did differ as a function of the race in which they chose to compete. These findings suggest that multiple participation options in an event will broaden the appeal of an event, but that an event's marketing communications can stress a common set of benefits.

The challenge for event marketers is to identify an appropriate set of benefits to promote. Recent work by Green and Chalip (1998b) demonstrates that the benefits event participants seek can be identified by reference to the sport's subculture. They build on work demonstrating that each sport develops a unique set of values and beliefs into which participants are socialised (e.g., Donnelly & Young, 1988; Kleiber & Kirshnit, 1991). Green and Chalip show that the opportunity to parade, celebrate, and share subcultural values and beliefs is a core attraction of a participative sport event. This finding suggests that an ideal means to market participative sport events is to identify the values and beliefs associated with the sport's subculture, and then to formulate marketing messages and images that communicate the opportunities the event will provide to parade, celebrate, and share those with other participants.

Future Directions

The considerations described above suggest that sport events need to be conceived of as more than mere sport. They need to be conceived in terms of the quality and kinds of experiences that those who attend (whether to participate or spectate) can obtain. This is more than a matter of providing good sport; it requires that the event offers an array of social and psychological benefits. The event manager must consider the event's spaces for formal and informal social interaction, the opportunities it provides for stories to be created and shared, the sense of festival it will impart, and the emotions and personal meanings it can elicit. These must be designed and marketed in a manner that is congruent with the values and beliefs of the target sport subculture.

Attention to these matters will optimise the event's appeal to spectators and participants. Spectators and participants, however, are not the only stakeholders by whom the event manager will be held accountable. Public officials, community residents, sponsors, and sport administrators may each have particular outcomes they seek from the event. Economic return, community pride, market reach, and sport development are likely to be among their objectives. Thus, the task of managing an event is also one of managing multiple stakeholders and multiple objectives.

The event management literature has, until recently, been focused entirely on instrumental concerns – on the requisites for providing good sport and good sport marketing. The literature has been surprisingly devoid of insight into the ways that event design can be used to foster (or to hinder) particular experiences for those who attend. Nor has it systematically examined the ways that different objectives can (or should) affect the tasks that event managers undertake or the alliances they form. Neither has it considered the particular challenges of managing multiple stakeholders, each with different agendas.

This chapter began by noting that events play a central role in the development of sport. The quality of the contribution that events make to sport development will depend, in part, on the degree to which matters of experience, objectives, and stakeholders are built into event design and production. These are the core challenges for the future. Additional research in these areas remains necessary to understand all aspects and impacts of events and devise lessons for design and implementation in event management.

References

Biddle, S.J.H. (1995). Exercise motivation across the lifespan. In S.J.H. Biddle (Ed.) *European perspectives on exercise and sport psychology* (pp. 3-25.) Champaign, IL: Human Kinetics.

Brooks, C.M. (1998). Sport/exercise identity theory and participation marketing: Theory formation and theoretical justification. *Sport Marketing Quarterly, 7(1),* 38-47.

Chalip, L. (1992). The construction and use of polysemic structures: Olympic lessons for sport marketing, *Journal of Sport Management, 6,* 87-98.

Chalip, L., Green, B.C., & Vander Velden, L. (1998). Sources of interest in travel to the Olympic Games, *Journal of Vacation Marketing, 4,* 7-22.

Cuskelly, G., McIntyre, N., & Boag, A. (1998). A longitudinal study of the development of organizational commitment amongst volunteer sport administrators. *Journal of Sport Management, 12,* 181-202.

Donnelly, P., & Young, K. (1988). The construction and confirmation of identity in sport subcultures, *Sociology of Sport Journal, 5,* 223-240.

Farrell, J.M., Johnston, M.E., & Twynam, G.D. (1998). Volunteer motivation, satisfaction, and management at an elite sporting competition. *Journal of Sport Management, 12,* 288-300.

Getz, D. (1998). Trends, strategies, and issues in sport-event tourism. *Sport Marketing Quarterly, 7(2),* 8-13.

Gladden, J.M., McDonald, M.A., & Barr, C.A. (1998). Event management. In L.P. Masteralexis, C.A. Barr, and M.A. Hums (Eds.), *Principles and practice of sport management* (pp. 328-355). Gaithersburg, MD: Aspen.

Goldfine, B., & Schleppi, J. (1997). Events. In M. Walker & D.K. Stotlar, *Sport Facility Management.* Sudbury, MA: Jones and Bartlett.

Green, B.C., & Chalip, L. (1998a). Sport volunteers: Research agenda and application. *Sport Marketing Quarterly, 7(2),* 14-23.

Green, B.C. & Chalip, L. (1998b). Sport tourism as the celebration of subculture, *Annals of Tourism Research, 25,* 275-291.

Guttmann, A. (1986). *Sports spectators.* New York: Columbia University Press.

Hall, C.M. (1992). *Hallmark tourist events: Impacts, management and planning.* London: Belhaven Press.

Kahle, L.R., Kambara, K.M., & Rose, G.M. (1996). A functional model of fan attendance motivations for college football, *Sport Marketing Quarterly, 5(4),* 51-60.

Kleiber, D.A., & Kirshnit, C.E. (1991). Sport involvement and identity formation. In L. Diamant (Ed.) *Mind-body maturity* (pp. 193-211). New York: Hemisphere Publishing.

Madrigal, R. (1995). Cognitive and affective determinants of fan satisfaction with sporting event attendance, *Journal of Leisure Research, 27,* 205-227.

Melnick, M.J. (1993). *Searching for sociability in the stands: A theory of sports spectating, 7,* 44-60.

Reiss, G. (1995). *Project management demystified (2nd ed.).* London: E & FN Spon.

Scanlan, T.K., & Simons, J. (1992). The construct of sport enjoyment. In G.C. Roberts (Ed.) *Motivation in sport and exercise* (pp. 199-215). Champaign, IL: Human Kinetics.

Tanabe, L., Green, B.C., & Chalip, L. (1998). Target marketing of sport events with multiple competitions: Lessons from the Gold Coast Marathon. In B. Faulkner, C. Tidswell & D. Weaver (Eds.) *Progress in tourism and hospitality research: Part 2* (pp. 441-442). Canberra: Bureau of Tourism Research.

van den Berg, L., Braun, E., & Otgaar, A.H.J. (2000). *Sports and city marketing in European cities.* Rotterdam: euricur.

Wankel, L.M. (1993). The importance of enjoyment to adherence and psychological benefits from physical activity. *International Journal of Sport Psychology, 24,* 151-169.

Whitson, D., & Macintosh, D. (1996). The global circus: International sport, tourism, and the marketing of cities, *Journal of Sport and Social Issues, 20,* 278-297.

Non-specialist Bibliography

American Sport Education Program (1996). *Event management for SportDirectors*. Champaign, IL: Human Kinetics.

Graham, S., Goldblatt, J.J., & Delpy, L. (1995). *The ultimate guide to sport event management & marketing*. Chicago: Irwin.

Gunsten, P.H. (1978). *Tournament scheduling the easy way*. Winsten-Salem, NC: Hunter Textbooks.

McDonnell, I., Allen, J., & O'Toole, W. (1999). *Festival and special event management*. Brisbane, Australia: John Wiley & Sons.

McMullen, L. (1988). Sport on brink of new era. *Marketing*, (January 14), 22-23.

Schreiber, A.L., & Lenson, B. (1994). *Lifestyle & event marketing: Building the new customer partnership*. New York: McGraw-Hill.

VOLUNTEERS

Issues Concerning Volunteerism and Paid Professionals

Karin J. Buchholz

Introduction

In today's competitive business environment, it has become increasingly more important to manage the bottom line and maximize resources in order to survive. Companies are forced to do more with less. This is true in the private sector, government organizations and the non-profit world. Given this focus and pressure on organizations to cut expenses and optimize resources, many companies are looking at ways to increase capacity through the effective use of volunteers and paid professionals. This chapter will give the reader ideas on how to organize a comprehensive plan utilizing volunteers and paid professionals, using a model devised effectively in the United States of America.

Identifying Need

As a new organization is formed, it is critical that senior staff create a strategic plan to outline the mission, vision, objectives and goals of the company. Through this process, an organization will get a better understanding of what resources will be needed to achieve its objectives. This needs assessment must address staffing requirements to identify the number of people the organization will need to hire and whether they will require volunteer assistance.

Correspondence to: Karin J. Buchholz, International Relations, United States Olympic Committee, One Olympic Plaza, Colorado Springs, CO 80909, USA, Tel: +1 719 578-4833, E-mail: Karin.Buchholz@usoc.org

Volunteers can be a very important pool of labor especially for nonprofit organizations, saving an organization a great deal of money. Although volunteers may not be paid monetarily, they do not come without a cost. Successful volunteer programs require a lot of time, effort and creativity. Organizations who plan ahead and work to develop a volunteer management program may have to dedicate a staff person or team to this process. However, the organization should see great dividends in its future.

The most important asset of an organization is its people. It takes passion, commitment, desire drive and intelligence from people who believe in the mission of the organization to make it successful. Therefore, it is vital to find the best and most qualified employees and volunteers to work for the agency. After finding the right team, the human resources staff or volunteer managers must work extremely hard to keep these people happy, satisfied and motivated. "Human resources is concerned not only with finding good leaders but also with forming a group of people with different skills who work congenially together for a common goal" (Wilbur et al., 2000). When an organization can do this, the chances of it being successful increase tremendously.

Human resources and volunteer management activities revolve around six broad categories:
  I.   Risk Management
  II.   Recruitment (addressing: compelling mission, the need, why people do not volunteer, targeted & non-targeted recruitment, virtual volunteering, job descriptions, interviewing, screening applicants, volunteer orientation)
  III.   Training and Development
  IV.   Evaluation and Feedback
  V.   Rewarding and Recognizing
  VI.   Future Direction & Trends

I. Risk Management

When developing a risk management and insurance program, an organization should consult an attorney who specializes in Federal and State Laws that govern corporations and non-profits. An insurance specialist should also be consulted to create a plan that addresses the organization's specific needs.

At the very least, an organization must be aware of and understand:
1. *Liabilities related to governance* – operating within the by-laws, including duty of care, loyalty and diligence.
2. *Operational liabilities of the agency* – Anticipating and planning for things that can go wrong while performing the duties of the organization.
3. *Compliance with Federal and State legislation and regulations* – e.g., Title VII of the Civil Rights Act of 1964 which, outlaws discrimination in employment practices toward individuals based on age, race, religion, sex, color or national origin.

(Wilbur et al., 2000)

II. Recruitment of Personnel

Again, the organization is only as good as its staff. People make organizations successful. Recruiting and hiring the right staff and volunteers is critical. Since most organizations have clear guidelines and strategies for hiring staff, this section focuses on recruiting volunteers for organizations. Many of the suggestions can apply to hiring paid professional as well.

Eight Keys to Successful Volunteer Recruitment Programs:
- Have a compelling mission
- Identify the need & match the person to the job
- Understand why people do not volunteer
- Have a targeted & non-targeted recruitment plan
- Virtual volunteering
- Create job descriptions & responsibilities
- Screen applicants
- Volunteer orientation

Have a Compelling Mission

Having a compelling mission is critical, especially for non-profit organizations. Most people who volunteer want to make a difference and will give up their spare time if they are motivated by the organization's mission. The recruiter/employer must be aware of the public's perception of the organization, whether it is good or bad, since this will affect their ability to recruit volunteers. The organization should have an excellent reputation, be well known and be visible in the community to optimize the quality and quantity volunteer pool. If the organization does not have a good reputation, it must focus on redefining itself and shifting the negative attitude. Part of the organization's strategy should be to get as much positive publicity about the organization to attract potential volunteers.

Identify the need & match person to the job

After you have identified a need for volunteer support, the organization should identify the type of person or the particular skills a person would need to help them achieve their goals. The Girl Scouts of America created a brochure that asked specific questions about the likes and dislikes of a person to match the job to the person and vice versa. An example of the brochure follows.

There is one that is right for you!		
If you like to :	*Then you would like being:*	*If you could give:*
Have fun with children	Troop Leader/Co Leader	A few hours a week
Plan and carry on activities	Day Camp Leader	A few weeks in Summer
Work as part of a team	Specialized Camp Leader	A few weeks in Summer
Teach simple games, songs crafts	Special Event Leader	A long day or weekend
If you're interested in:	*Then you'd be interested in:*	*If you could give:*
Meeting a variety of people	Troop Organizer	Many hours for 2-3 month period
Speaking to a group of adults	Volunteer Recruiter	Many hours for 2-3 month period
Finding out about your community	Nominating Committee Member	A few hours weekly for 2-3 months

If you can:	Then you could be:	If you could give:
Work toward goals	District/Neighborhood Chairperson	Several hours weekly
Coordinate participation	Day Camp/Special Camp Director	Many hours for 2-3 month period
Conduct effective meeting	Event Director	Many hours for 2-3 month period
If you are good at:	**Then you would be good at:**	*If you could give:*
Following through on detail	Cookie/Calendar Chairperson	Many hours for 2-3 month period
Keeping records or accounts	District Training Registrar	Many hours for 2 month period
Making telephone contacts	Secretary for Neighborhood/District	A few hours a month
Completing reports	Day Camp Business Manager	Many hours for 2 months
If you're able to:	**Then you could be:**	**If you could give:**
Analyze information	Board Member	Several hours quarterly
Set direction and priorities	Committee Member	Several hours monthly
Assess support or evaluate programs	Special task group member	Many hours for 2-3 month period

Whichever volunteer position you choose, girls will benefit.
Call to volunteer: 241-1270, EXT. 269

Understand why people do not volunteer

Before starting the recruitment process, it is important to understand why people do not volunteer. A volunteer management program can address those barriers and provide a valuable and worthwhile experience for all volunteers.

Reasons Why People Do not Volunteer	Ways to address issues
1. No one asked	Ask them!!!
2. Do not have time	Make the project manageable Explore virtual volunteering
3. Lack of confidence to do a job	Provide volunteer orientation, training and development
4. Lack of experience with an organization	Provide potential volunteers with testimonials; invite respected supporters of the organization to recruit
5. Fear of long term commitment	Break projects up into manageable pieces
6. Negative image of an organization	Initiate a positive public relations campaign

Findings Reported in the 1996 publication of Giving and Volunteering in the United States of America:

- In 1995, 48.8% of the population volunteered (about 93 million people). Volunteers gave an average of 4.2 hours per week.
- When asked how they learned about their volunteering activities, people said, 1) they were asked by someone, 2) through participation in an organization, 3) that a family member or relative would benefit
- 85% of people, who were asked to volunteer, did. Members of religious organizations were more likely to be asked to volunteer than non-members.
- 70.7% of college graduates volunteer. 43% of high school graduates volunteer.

(Source: Giving and Volunteering in the United States: Findings from a National Survey, conducted in 1996 by the Gallup Organization for Independent Sector)

Being aware of these findings can help an organization target specific people for positions.

Have a targeted and non-targeted recruitment plan

There are two basic methods of planning a recruitment program: Non-targeted and targeted.

1. *Targeted recruitment* is specific and focused. It is targeted toward groups of people with specific skills, interests and talents. Depending on the need of the organization, the recruiter must narrow his/her target. Examples include:
   - Specific trade organizations
   - Volunteer organizations – Americorp, Vista Volunteers
   - Service organizations or clubs
   - Corporate newsletters
   - College placement centers
   - Marketing volunteer opportunities online - the Internet offers unique ways to recruit volunteers with specific skills

2. *Non-targeted recruitment* is broad based. This form of recruitment works best when:

- A large number of volunteers is needed for a clean-up day or a large event
- The job does not require any specific skills or a lengthy commitment

Recruiting in these situations calls for a wide distribution of information. Such as:
- Posters & flyers in public settings – supermarkets, laundromats, bookstores, college dorms, etc.
- Local newspapers
- Radio shows or public service announcements (PSAs)
- Internet new groups and lists. Excellent places to find appropriate newsgroups include:
  - <www.liszt.com>
  - <www.lsoft.com/catalis.html>
  - <www.tile.net>
  - <http://DiscussionLists.com/>
  - <www.neosoft.com/cgi-bin/paml_search/>
  - <www.Remarq.com>
  - <www.dejanews.com>
  (Ellis, 1994; Bower, 2000)

It is vital to use all available resources to find volunteers. Reasons to recruit online are:
1. It is fast, cost effective, and easy.
2. It is an excellent way to reach non-traditional volunteers and populations that are under-represented in an organization.
3. Ability to reach a very targeted market, such as a particular type of profession.

Although recruitment seems to be an overwhelming, year round task, there are several ways to make the job easier. Remember to:
- Take advantage of an existing network – look to friends, co-workers, family members, the local community, neighbors, clients, etc.
- Enter into collaborations and partnerships – this could be with colleges or universities, other organizations, youth groups, etc.
- Share recruitment work with others – churches, corporations, and other groups that already have methods of mobilizing and supervising volunteers.

- Create joint marketing and public relations opportunities, particularly with an area business.
- Create links on other companies' Web pages.

(Ellis, 1994)

Job Descriptions

When the hiring process begins, it is best to start with a precise written job description. This job description will serve as a barometer for such activities as promotions, performance appraisals and salary increases. While job descriptions should be reviewed at least once a year, they should also be revisited if there is any shift in employee responsibility. (Wilbur et al., 2000)

There is much to learn from today's volunteer workforce when looking for volunteer positions within an organization. Try to make volunteer opportunities as diverse as possible. Different types of people are drawn to different types of jobs, volunteers will search for job opportunities that enable them to use their current strengths as well as learn new skills. <www.serviceleader.org>

Components of a good job description:

- Position Title – it should reflect the volunteer's responsibilities and help others understand their role in the organization
- Location – where the job will be located – can it be a virtual volunteering opportunity?
- Volunteer Impact – outline how the completion of the job or project will contribute to the overall mission of the organization. Show the volunteer how important and vital their role in the organization is, regardless of the responsibilities and duties assigned. Everyone's job contributes to the success of the organization.
- Responsibilities & Duties – clear goals and objectives provide the volunteer with a road map. Provide a list of tasks that must be performed or a clear description of the desired outcome. List both the expectations of the person and the job.
- Qualifications – list the characteristics, qualities, work experience and education required to perform the job in the best possible way.
- Commitment Required – this is one of the most important aspects of a good job description. Most people want to know how long their

services will be needed. Short term projects attract more people. Be sure to have a start and end date for the project or job.

- Training – if applicable – list the training opportunities and requirements for the job.
- Supervisor – let them know whom they will be directly reporting to.
- Probation Period & Evaluation – let them know up front how they will be evaluated and let them know that they will be on probation for a specified period of time to evaluated.

Screening

This area is critical. If not taken seriously, it can ruin an organization. All applicants must be screened before being considered for the position. Many organizations are desperate for help and are grateful and often surprised when people express an interest in volunteering. This desperation can cause an organization to accept whomever walks through the front door. Just because you have a "warm body" who wants to volunteer, doesn't mean you have to accept them. Be very selective, the volunteer will represent the organization and the agency can be held liable for any actions of that person.

Screening Tips:
1. Start with a volunteer application form and design it carefully.
2. Conduct a criminal background check – this can be useful in two ways: a) Many criminal offenders will withdraw their applications if they know the organization conducts mandatory background checks, b) Many offenders leave their states or communities to volunteer in other areas, the background check can help identify who they are.
3. Check references and call people who are not on their reference list.
4. Use your "gut" when it comes to character judgements. If someone doesn't "feel" right, do not take the chance.

Interviewing

As in the hiring process for a paid position, the interview is a critical component of recruitment. Both the interviewer and the candidate have the opportunity to assess each other and decide whether there is a fit.

Interviewing Tips:
1. Use indirect questions such as:
    - What brings you here?
    - What jobs have you held in the past that you've like the most? Why?
    - What jobs have you held that you disliked? Why?
    - Describe a perfect supervisor for you.
    - What do you consider the greatest challenges you have faced and how did you handle them?
    - What are the most difficult decisions you've had to make?
    - What do you see yourself doing with us?
    - What do you expect from your work with us?
2. Make sure your interview time is uninterrupted.
3. Be an active listener and do not talk too much.
4. Answer any questions honestly and openly.
5. Listen to your "gut reactions". If an answer sounds odd, pursue it.
6. Be friendly.
7. If they have objections, work to discover what they are and remove them if possible.
8. Never promise what you can't deliver.
9. Remove their reasons to say "NO".
10. Try to assess what needs and motivation they have and match them in your mind to jobs that can meet those same motivations.
11. Never assume anything.

Volunteer Orientation Session

Volunteering for a new organization can be intimidating. The best way to alleviate a lot of the anxiety felt by a new volunteer is to have a comprehensive orientation session before the job begins. Part of the orientation process should include introductions to all staff and other volunteers. Most often this orientation will help the volunteer feel a part of the team and help them see how their service will contribute to the overall success of the organization.

Topics to Cover in a Volunteer Orientation Session
1. Description and history of the organization
2. Description of programs and participants

3. How the organization relates to the community and to other organizations
4. Description of the volunteer program
5. Sketch of an organizational chart and introduction of key staff
6. Timeline of major organizational events throughout the year
7. Introduction of volunteer manual on policies and procedures
8. Facilities orientation: office layout, phones, restrooms, parking, meals, coffee, etc.
9. Outline of volunteer benefits
10. Notification of volunteer training schedule
11. Introduction of supervisory system and personnel
12. Description of procedures to follow in case of an emergency
13. Description of performance appraisal and review system
14. Opportunities for growth and job development

Virtual Volunteer

As more and more people work from home, there is also an increasing trend for people to do their volunteer work via the Internet or from their home office. Virtual volunteering allows a person to dedicate their time and contribute their expertise without having to be physically present. For more information, contact <www.serviceleader.org>.

III. Training & Development

This area can never be over-emphasized. One of the goals of an organization should be to invest in human capital, since quality people create quality agencies. Training and development opportunities give all staff and volunteers the tools they need to succeed. Many people volunteer to gain valuable "on the job" experience. The volunteer manager should make sure there are numerous opportunities for growth and development. This contributes to volunteer retention as well.

Training can be formal or informal. Formal training includes classes, seminars and conferences. Informal training includes on the job training with a mentor or by trial and error. Whether the education is formal or informal, constantly providing volunteers with growth opportunities will pay dividends in the long run for any organization.

IV. Evaluation

Every employer and volunteer needs feedback on how they are doing. Periodic feedback from the supervisor will contribute to the learning and development of the volunteer. Evaluations can be based on the job description, on goals set by the supervisor and volunteer, or on the progress of a particular project.   While feedback should happen often, a formal evaluation only needs to take place 2-4 times per year.   After a formal evaluation, the supervisor and the volunteer should celebrate successes as well as identify ways to improve and learn from mistakes. It should always be a positive experience, even when results are negative, and used as a learning opportunity for both parties.

Evaluation Tips
- Assess actions, not people or personalities
- Give the volunteer a blank evaluation form prior to the meeting and ask them to evaluate their own performance
- Make evaluations honest and clear
- Give evaluations (especially those to correct action) as immediately as possible
- Phrase evaluations positively, not negatively
- Develop evaluation comments through varied perspectives
- Document all evaluations
- Give volunteers clear written guidelines (job design, goals, desired results) of what is to be accomplished to be used in the evaluation
- At checkpoints during work and at completion:
  - Review goals and progress toward these goals
  - Identify strongest aspects and how to continue to duplicate them in the future
  - Identify problems and how to avoid them in the future
  - Sketch out plans for the next evaluation
  - Celebrate successes and learning
  - Ask them how you as supervisor could better support them in the future
  - Note assistance that could have helped along the way
- Avoid grading system of "great", "ok", "yuck". Substitute "superior", "fine", "could benefit from further training". Everyone likes to be a winner.

- Be realistic
- When holding a group or committee assessment of completed work, keep the dialogue positive – ask the participants to identify things that worked well and opportunities to improve: do not dwell on "good" or "bad".

(Vineyard, 1999)

V. Reward & Recognition

"Volunteer managers need to satisfy the interests and needs of prospective volunteers, who, like discriminating customers, can choose from a multitude of alternatives in the volunteer marketplace. Simply having a worthwhile cause and meaningful volunteer activities to offer are no longer sufficient." (Fisher, 1993, p. 81). That's why it is critical to accurately match volunteers to jobs, recognizing and rewarding their accomplishments.

It is also important to provide volunteers with a list of benefits they will derive from their service. Identifying what motivates a person to volunteer will help you design the appropriate reward, recognition and benefits that are to be received. Everyone is different and individually motivated by different reasons. Make sure they have opportunities to learn and grow.

Here are a few reasons people volunteer:
1. The need for achievement
2. The need for affiliation
3. The need for power
4. The need for growth & balance
5. The need for FUN
6. The need to serve and give back

Once it is known why a person is volunteering, an organization can tailor their rewards to satisfy the volunteer's needs. This increases the chances of the volunteer working with them again in the future.

Rewarding Tips
For Affiliation Motivated People:
- Recognize them in the presence of family and friends
- Provide them with social opportunities to make new friends

- Give them assignments with a lot of personal contact
- Put their names in the newsletter so other people can see their role

For Power Motivated People:
- Give them jobs that allow them to persuade others
- Give them jobs that allow them to interact with the highest authorities
- Give them impressive job titles
- Invite them to serve on the board

For Achievement Motivated People:
- Give them opportunities to give input in goal related decisions
- Assign entire projects to them
- Give them tangible awards, plaques, etc.
- Be careful not to waste their time

(Vineyard, 1984)

VI. Future Direction and Trends

All effective managers are successful because they learn from the past, live in the present and plan for the future. They are masters at scanning their environment for clues about the future and refining and improving their organizations to remain competitive in their industry.

Recruiting trends in the industry

- Greater demand for short-term or episodic volunteering for a variety of reasons.   If you have a long-term project, try breaking it up into manageable pieces of short term opportunities.
- Family Volunteering – Many people want to give back and volunteer their time, but not at the expense of losing quality time with their families. Organizations should explore the possibility of providing opportunities for the entire family to volunteer. (Ellis, Weisbord, & Noyes, 1991; Thurmond & Cassell, 1996.)
- College Volunteers and Interns – "about 25% of American Colleges and dozens of high schools have recently instituted volunteer work in the curriculum" (Brudney, 1990, p. 161, full citation). Most universities and other educational institutions have offices that coordinate student activities and service projects. (Lowenthal, Tarnoff & David, 1995)

Demographic Trends:
- Aging baby boomers – as this generation ages and has more time on their hands, organizations can target them for volunteer positions
- Greater ethnic diversity – these new faces can help diversify an organization
- Sandwich generation - individuals who have been squeezed by the needs of their children and aging parents, will volunteer if the organization is flexible. Try virtual volunteering or family volunteering.

Work style and work value trends:
- The fact that two parents are now working leaves little time for volunteering. Try virtual or family volunteering in this case.
- The increase in the number of people working from home, make them prime candidates for virtual volunteering and family volunteering as well.
- Sequencing in and out of the job market, particularly with women, adds a lot of people who are between jobs to the volunteer pool.
- People who have retired early, whether it be forced and voluntary, make them a perfect group to target.

Educational Trends:
- Educational institutions requiring service learning
- Need for internships for work experience
- Frequent training and re-training necessary during the lifetime of employment.

Conclusion

As mentioned previously, an organization must effectively manage its human resources to be successful. Organizations that put the time and effort into creating worthwhile employee and volunteer management programs and who focus on the six areas outlined in this chapter, will improve their competitiveness and achieve their goals more effectively. This model has been used successfully throughout programs of the United States Olympic Committee where volunteers have made the difference.

References

Bower, J. (2000, November 26). Personal correspondence. United States Olympic Committee, Volunteer Manager.

Ellis, S.J. (1994). *The Volunteer Recruitment Book, 2nd ed.* New York, NY: Knopf Publishers.

Ellis, S.; Weisbord, A.; Noyes, K. (1991). *Children as Volunteers: Preparing for Community Service.* Philadelphia: Energize.

Fisher, J.C. (1993). *Leadership and Management of Volunteer Programs.* San Francisco: Jossey-Bass, p. 8

Giving & Volunteering in the United States: Findings from a National Survey, conducted in 1996 by the Gallup Organization for independent Sector.

Lowenthal, P.; Tarnoff, S.; David, L. (Eds.). (1995). *Recruiting College Volunteers: A Guide for Volunteer Recruitment and Management.* Big Brothers/Big Sisters of America.

Nonprofit Risk Management Center, 1001 Connecticut Avenue, NW, Washington, DC 20036 <www.nonprofitrisk.org>

Thurmond, D.P.; Cassell, J. (1996). *Family Volunteering: Putting the Pieces Together.* The Points of Light Foundation.

Vineyard, S. (1993). *Megatrends* & *Volunteerism: Mapping the Future for Volunteer Programs.* New York, NY: Heritage Arts Publications.

Vineyard, S. (1999). *Evaluating Volunteer, Programs and Events and Reflection; The Evaluative Component of Service-Learning.* Madison, WI: Glencoe/MacMillan/McGraw Hill.

Vineyard, S. (1984). *Beyond Banquets, Plaques and Pins: Creative Ways to Recognize Volunteers and Staff! New York,* NY: McKnight Publishing Co.

Wilbur, R.H.; Bucklin, S., Smith, A. (2000). *The Complete Guide to Nonprofit Management.* New York, NY: Wiley & Sons.

DEVELOPING THE BUSINESS OF SPORT IN ASIA

Public Sport and Recreation in Hong Kong

Kian Lam Toh

Introduction

In terms of economy, not many people would classify Hong Kong under the category of "developing country". In terms of sport business however, not many people would deny that Hong Kong is still a developing territory in spite of the fact that numerous major international sporting events have been organized annually in the territory. Hong Kong regularly hosts a number of major international sporting events. The Carlsberg Cup Soccer tournament is normally held during the Chinese New Year holidays in either January or February. This year, the national teams of Mexico, Czech Republic and Japan played against the elite of Hong Kong Football for the prestigious cup. The Hong Kong Marathon is held every February. This event has earned international status in recent years and has become so popular that more than 7,000 runners participated in 1999. In March, the world-famous Rugby Sevens comes to the territory. The exciting three-day tournament, Hong Kong's most popular single international sporting event, always manages to draw tens of thousands of paying fans. Also in March, the Hong Kong International Golden Mile (running) attracts many distance runners from around the region and the world. In October, many professional tennis players gather here for the CMGI Asia Open (ATP tour). As for the legendary men's tennis players, they assemble here in November for the Cathay Pacific Championship (Hong Kong Tourist Association, 1999).

Correspondence to: Dr. Kian Lam Toh, Assistant Professor, Department of Physical Education, Hong Kong Baptist University, R5-116, 34 Renfrew Road, Kowloon Tong, Kowloon, Hong Kong. E-mail: kltoh@hkbu.edu.hk

Interest in the business of sport has expanded at an exponential rate in recent years in many countries around the world. Hong Kong is no exception. In fact, the Hong Kong Government has been quite supportive in this regard. This is evident by the establishment of a bidding committee for hosting the 2006 Asian Games, headed by the Chief Secretary of the Hong Kong Special Administrative Region (HKSAR).

The scope of sport business can be very broad. Sport organizations such as sporting goods companies, professional sport teams, private sport and fitness clubs, public agencies that provide sport programs and so forth are all parts of the sport business. Since it is impossible to discuss every aspect of it, this paper will only focus on the provision of a general picture of public sport and recreation in Hong Kong.

Hong Kong is one of the model examples in Asia that has a proven record of providing public sport and recreation opportunities for its people. The Leisure and Cultural Services Department (LCSD) is the main provider of public sport and recreation locally. Other providers include YMCAs, local sport and recreation clubs and the like. They will not be included in the discussion of this paper because of the length limit. With regard to the training of elite athletes, it is the responsibility of the Hong Kong Sports Development Board (SDB).

The standards and guidelines for recreation and open space planning have been delineated clearly in governmental documents (Hong Kong Planning Standards and Guidelines, 1998). It is very significant and important to have these documents because they help protect the public's rights to participate in sport and recreation. The standards of provision for core activities, the standard dimensions of facilities for core activities and the standards of provision for recreation buildings all help ensure that the general public has sufficient facilities for sport endeavors.

Sport participation among Hong Kong people has been increasing steadily during the past few years. In 1998, an average of 54% of the adult population (aged 15 or above) participated in at least one sport activity. The sport participation rate for 1996 and 1997 was 40% and 50% respectively (Hong Kong Sports Development Board, 1999). Based on the fact that there were 5.65 million adults aged 15 or above in 1998, it represented a total sporting population of 3.05 million. That figure did not include those below the age of 15. On the other hand, the number of public sport and recreation programs has increased from 900 in 1974 to 20,982 in March 2000 (P. Cheung, personal communication, March 17, 2000). These figures all strongly imply the strong potential for sport business in Hong Kong. The inclusion of this topic would provide a better understanding about the business of public sport and recreation in the Pearl of the East.

Historical Development

The development of sport and recreation in Hong Kong can be traced back for more than a half century. After World War II, Hong Kong began to recover from the aftermath of the war and developed rapidly to become one of the most famous business centers in the world. People's incomes increased drastically because of the rapid economic growth and they started to demand more sport and recreation opportunities with a view to achieve a higher quality of life.

The year 1967 can be used as a dividing line for the organized public sport and recreation programs in Hong Kong. Before 1967, the government provided very limited sport and recreation activities for the public. Most of the activities were played at private clubs such as the Royal Hong Kong Jockey Club and the Hong Kong Cricket Club, just to name a couple. The main reason for the government to change its view towards the provision of public sport and recreation was the riot that took place in 1967. After that incident, the government started to realize that the youngsters should be given proper guidance to develop their ethical minds and characters. They should be encouraged to participate in more sport and recreation activities in their leisure time. The governmental departments including Education, Social Welfare, Police Forces, Agricultural and Fisheries, Urban Council and other voluntary agencies joined together to provide more public sport and recreation programs for the people of Hong Kong. The National Sports Associations (NSAs) were also encouraged to assist the government in developing sport to meet the needs of the Hong Kong people.

The Council for Recreation and Sport (CRS), headed by the Secretary for Home Affairs and comprised of appointed members from the various governing sports bodies and the business industries, was established in

October 1973, to advise "the government on the provision and usage of facilities, expenditure of government funds, supervision of voluntary and government agencies in the promotion of recreation and sports and recommendations on special services and facilities required to meet the leisure needs of the young people of Hong Kong" (Mak, 1999, p. 37). Another main task of the CRS was to provide financial support to the NSAs. In addition, the Recreation and Sports Service (RSS), housed under the Education Department, was set up in 1974, as recommended by the CRS. The role of the RSS was to promote sport and recreation activities to all ages with particular focus on youngsters. During its first year of operation, the RSS, which only operated in six districts, had promoted 900 programs that attracted some 130,000 participants. Due to the success, the government decided to expand the service to all 17 districts the following year.

However, the expanded RSS faced many problems especially in terms of facilities. That was mainly because the Urban Council, which managed all the urban sport facilities, maintained that only a small quota of the facilities would be allocated to the programs offered by RSS. As a result, programs and events were even conducted in school playgrounds, unused warehouses, rooftops and car parks (Mak, 1999). In 1982, the RSS broke away from the Education Department and found its new home with the newly established Recreation and Culture Department. Lack of facilities however, still continued to be a major problem for the same reason described earlier.

Fortunately, the Regional Council was established in 1985, to provide recreation and sport programs and facilities for the residents living in the New Territories*. At the same time, the Recreation and Culture Department was disbanded and the recreation and sport programs of the RSS were transferred to the Urban Council. The concern about the facilities was thus eliminated and both the councils continued to provide Sport-For-All programs at the district level for all the people of Hong Kong. In 1999 alone, more than 1.1 million people participated in the sport and recreation programs provided by the two councils. The funds allocated for both the councils during the same period of time amounted to HK$84 million. Tables 1

---

*HKSAR is basically divided into three main areas, Hong Kong Island, Kowloon, and the New Territories which also include various out-lying islands.

and 2 illustrate the number of projects, participants and the funds allocated for the Urban and Regional Councils respectively from 1986 to 1999.

Year	No. of Projects	No. of Participants	Allocation (HK$m)
1986-87	4,228	195,607	4.9
1987-88	5,442	220,195	6.4
1988-89	6,703	240,399	7.2
1989-90	7,371	253,014	9.1
1990-91	7,935	254,784	10.2
1991-92	8,218	287,456	14.3
1992-93	6,970	328,738	12.9
1993-94	7,487	366,430	18.1
1994-95	7,821	410,712	23.3
1995-96	8,356	500,821	26.5
1996-97	8,811	532,860	31.6
1997-98	9,360	646,293	41.8
1998-99	9,956	656,700	48.8

Table 1: District Sport and Recreation Projects Organized by the Urban Council from 1986 – 1999

The Urban and Regional Councils were dissolved on January 1, 2000 and a new Leisure and Cultural Services Department (LCSD) was established on the same day. The main responsibility of the new department was to promote and deliver leisure and cultural services throughout the HKSAR.

Year	No. of Projects	No. of Participants	Allocation (HK$m)
1986-87	3,799	223,181	4.9
1987-88	4,164	211,318	5.1
1988-89	4,701	211,802	5.6
1989-90	4,939	210,561	7.1
1990-91	4,956	283,309	10.3
1991-92	5,065	211,152	10.0
1992-93	5,255	534,903	13.0
1993-94	5,455	297,810	13.2
1994-95	6,280	476,823	19.3
1995-96	7,183	404,856	21.3
1996-97	7,415	709,929	25.5
1997-98	7,883	457,549	30.6
1998-99	8,005	520,576	35.2

Table 2: District Sport and Recreation Projects Organized by the Regional Council from 1986 – 1999

The Status Quo

The former Urban and Regional Councils put their emphasis on the "Sport-For-All" concept. In other words, a wide range of sport and recreation activities were organized for the public and the participants were encouraged to take part in sport and recreation activities during their leisure time. The sport and recreation programs organized by the two Municipal Councils, and later the LCSD, together with the NSAs include skill learning and training at elementary and intermediate level for various racquet and team sports, aquatic and athletic activities, fitness and dance activities, and outdoor pursuits. Competitions and tournaments at the beginner level are also provided for the people who prefer to compete with others or to challenge themselves. In addition to the training-oriented programs, a comprehensive range of recreational activities is also available to meet the needs of all ages. These include children's sport and fun games, excursions, and family camps, just to name a few. A series of innovative programs have also been organized for the public to further increase their awareness about the benefits and values of sport and physical recreation. Special focus has also been put on encouraging the senior citizens, blue-collar workers and people with disabilities to be involved in sport and recreation. Should there be talented athletes, the NSAs concerned would continue to assist them in developing their potential through their own training and developmental programs with the assistance from the SDB.

Besides delivering various sport and recreation programs, the LCSD also provides a wide variety of sport facilities for the public. As mentioned earlier, the HKSAR provides sport facilities based on the "Standards of Provision for Recreation Buildings". For examples, there is an indoor games hall for every 25,000 – 49,999 residents and a standard swimming complex for every 287,000 residents. A list of the major sport and recreation facilities managed by the LCSD can be found in Table 3.

Sport & Recreational Facilities	Number
Beaches	36
Bowling Green	7
Children's Playgrounds	606
Golf Driving Ranges	3
Hard-surface Pitches (for mini-soccer, basketball, etc.)	224
Hockey Pitches	2
Indoor Games Halls	78
Indoor Stadia	2
Natural & Artificial Turf Pitches (for soccer)	67
Outdoor Stadia	2
Rugby Pitches	2
Sports Grounds	24
Squash Courts	322
Swimming Pool Complexes	33
Tennis Courts	273
Water Sports Centers	4

Table 3: Major Sport and Recreational Facilities Managed by the LCSD

"Fitness" concept

A new campaign on "Healthy Exercise for All" has been launched to encourage the public to do exercise for at least 30 minutes each day in order to keep fit. The NSAs will continue to be encouraged to organize more training programs with the financial support from the SDB. They have also been asked to select a venue as their training base called the National Squad Training Center and designated venues will be set aside for their use to develop their respective sport.

What does the future hold?

Public sport and recreation in Hong Kong have made significant progress in the last couple of decades. The demand for sport and recreation activities has increased tremendously due to improved economic conditions and standards of living, rapid development of modern facilities and urbanization, and perhaps shorter working hours. Hong Kong people are able to choose from a variety of sport and recreation activities provided mainly by the LCSD. The demand for sport and recreation programs and facilities will continue to grow in the coming years.

Although the future of sport and recreation in Hong Kong looks bright, sport still faces several challenges. Firstly, the new LCSD might not be able to maintain the same level of services for the public when compared with the former Urban and Regional Council. A government organization might not have the same resources and flexibility as those enjoyed by the two municipal councils (Mak, 1999). This is a big challenge because the public will expect improvements and will not want to settle for anything less.

Another challenge faced by the Government is to encourage the general public to build up a lifetime sport. They should be encouraged to pursue sport on their own rather than relying on the government's provision. This is achievable because thousands of people have already gone through the basic training programs provided by the two former municipal councils. The main task then is to develop a range of Regional Sports and Fitness Centers, like those in Singapore. These centers offer a full range of sport facilities that include a stadium with a running track and sport field, a swimming complex, a multi-purpose indoor sports hall, a gymnasium and fitness center, outdoor fitness stations, an aerobics studio and areas for social activities. They serve as community sport and recreation headquarters. New sport facilities could be constructed but these are not a must. Main emphasis should be placed on re-grouping the existing sport facilities that form the regional sport centers. These centers can continue to be manned by the professional staff of the LCSD. Self-initiated sport and recreation activities could also take place at these centers.

The third challenge will be to provide more sport and recreation opportunities for individuals with a disability. If possible, all the sport and recreation facilities should be renovated so that they are accessible to people with disabilities. Modification of sporting equipment and rules are also necessary to cater to the public's needs. Besides providing accessible facilities and programs, more instructors who are qualified to teach different sport skills to people with a disability are also desired. Similarly, provisions of appropriate sport and recreation activities and facilities for the elderly should not be ignored. After all, more than 10% of the total population in Hong Kong are at least 65 years of age.

Conclusion

In his 1999 Policy Address, the Chief Executive of the HKSAR, Mr. TUNG Chee Hwa outlined the picture of the development of Hong Kong in the 21st Century ("Policy Address 99," 1999). He highlighted the importance of supporting the extensive promotion of sport development so that the people of Hong Kong can enjoy vigorous health and colorful community life. The HKSAR Government will strive to enhance the quality of the local sporting environment through the provision of more sport and recreational facilities. Efforts will also be put into fostering more exchanges in sport with Mainland China and other parts of the world. With the assurance from the most powerful person in the HKSAR, the future of sport in the territory can only become brighter.

References

Hong Kong Planning Standards and Guidelines. (1998). *Recreation and open space.* Planning Department: Government of the Hong Kong Special Administrative Region.

Hong Kong Sports Development Board. (1999). *Sports participation survey 1998.* Research Department: Hong Kong Sports Development Board.

Hong Kong Sports Development Board. (1999). *Annual report 1998-99.*

Hong Kong Tourist Association. (1999). *Annual report 98/99.*

Jones, E.B. (1988). *The way ahead − A consultancy report on sport in Hong Kong.* Affairs Bureau: Hong Kong Government

Lam, A.C.C. (1999). *The consultant's report on culture, the arts, recreation and sports services.* Home Affairs Bureau: Government of the Hong Kong Special Administrative Region.

Mak, D. (1999). Recreation and sport development in Hong Kong − 25 years (1974 − 1999). *Journal of Physical Education & Recreation (Hong Kong),* 5(1), 36-42.

Policy address 99. (1999, October 7). *South China Morning Post,* p. VI-VII.

Woo, J. (1996). The changes in provision of recreation and sport services with the economic growth in Hong Kong. *Hong Kong Recreation Review,* 8, 35-40.

Internet Resources

Leisure & Cultural Services Department Quality Services for Quality Life, Hong Kong
<www.lcsd.gov.hk>

Hong Kong Sport Development Board
<www.hksdb.org.hk>

The Singapore Sports Council
<www.ssc.gov.sg>

WOMEN'S IMPACT ON SPORT

Donna A. Lopiano

Significance of Women in Previously All-Male Cultural Institutions

The entrance of women in the predominantly male cultural institutions of sport, the military and religion has created significant tension and change. Nowhere are social roles and symbols of status more well defined and ritualized than in these important societal activities. The uniforms and ranks, the honoring of those in the ruling hierarchy, the rigidity and stability of values and process and the perceived importance of these occupations are the subject of history and legend as well as current practice. Permitting women to access positions within these important institutions involves a transfer of real and perceived power of considerable magnitude. This transfer has occurred slowly and with great resistance from those currently in power within these institutions. Add this resistance to centuries of mythology regarding the mental and physical inferiority of women and the magnitude of the change challenge is very considerable.

For example, in religion, the prohibition of women as occupants of important religious positions is still the rule rather than the exception. Practising religious leadership does not require physical skill or strength. Rather, the root of male dominance lies in history and the supposed mandate of God, both of which are difficult to refute because God is not around to ask and religious interpretation still rests with those who would deny women religious leadership roles. In the case of the military, arguments have become less effective as war becomes less of a physical

Correspondence to: Dr. Donna Lopiano, Women's Sport Foundation, Eisenhower Park, East Meadow, NY 11554, USA.
E-mail: Wosportdl@aol.com

battle in the trenches and more technological. It is fascinating to listen to the reasons why women shouldn't fly airplanes in combat. Since there is no proof that they are less able to perform piloting and targeting skills, debate has sunk to the seeking of public support of exclusion from combat roles because of the prospect of rape if female pilots are captured (as if the same violation could not be inflicted upon male pilots).

Because of its physical nature, sport has been a particularly resistant cultural arena. Males who are, on the average, bigger, stronger and faster, dominate females in head-to-head competition. Thus, in many ways, sport symbolically reinforces stereotypical views of women's inferiority to men. It took an almost ludicrous sport exhibition on a world television stage, the Battle of the Sexes tennis match between Bobby Riggs and Billie Jean King in 1974, to shatter the common belief that women could not withstand extremes of psychological pressure in highly competitive settings. And, it takes considerable effort to get people to realize that bigger does not mean better. Who is the better athlete: Sugar Ray Leonard or Mike Tyson? The answer is neither because they compete in two different weight classes and it would not be fair competition for them to compete against each other. Both are great athletes. Similarly, Nancy Lopez should not be compared to Jack Nicklaus and Steffi Graf should not be matched against Pete Sampras. As obvious as this sounds, the public simply does not immediately grasp such distinctions and succumbs to the common belief that male athletes are better than female athletes.

As slow as acceptance into these predominantly male cultural institutions is, the sheer presence of women is extraordinarily significant. The attainment of position and respect in such highly visible, high status institutions makes an indelible mark on society. When women are performing important or revered roles, it is difficult to perpetuate stereotypical beliefs of inferiority. As their numbers increase, it becomes difficult to explain the achievements of women in these fields as exceptions.

Myths of Physical Inferiority

Historically, incredible arguments concerning the anatomical inferiority of women have been waged in the context of sport. Medical doctors (and others whom the public holds in high esteem and credibility) succumbed to mythology and continually failed to provide a balanced perspective on female health and injury. In the late 1800s, when women were emancipated from the home by the bicycle, there were doctors who wrote in respected medical journals of the dreaded disease "bicycle face." Imagining the pain of a female sitting astride a bicycle, they warned of a wrinkled face response and the permanence of such disfigurement. The effect of such warnings was to keep women away from this recreational sport. And, symbolically, the supposed physical inferiority of women in sport, was extended to the mental and physical abilities of women to withstand the stresses of highly competitive business environments.

In the 1920s, following the first running of the women's 800 meters in the Olympic Games, an irresponsible journalist erroneously reported that all 11 runners had collapsed. In fact, nine ran, all nine finished and one fell at the finish. Medical doctors followed with cautions about the lack of aerobic capabilities of women due to their smaller hearts, lungs and circulatory capacities and the event was dropped from the Olympic program. It was not until the 1950s that a women's running event over 200 meters was reintroduced to the Games.

Throughout the 1930s, medical doctors warned that high stress sport would negatively impact a female's reproductive system. In the 1980s and 1990s, medical doctors warned the public about eating disorders and the female athlete triad (eating disorders/osteoporosis/amenorrhea), which affected female athletes in the image sports of figure skating, gymnastics and diving. In the 1990s, medical doctors suggested hormonal differences and suggested that a woman's "Q angle" (angle between hip and knee) was a causative anatomical deficiency as the popular media heralded anterior cruciate injuries as the new scourge in women's sports. Thus, it has taken almost a century of intellectual battle and defeat of medical arguments to produce a major expansion of women's participation of sport and widespread public acceptance of the female as an athlete.

Career Limiting Sex Role Stereotypes

In particular, the expanded role of women in sport over the last quarter century in the United States has generated the necessary proof that women are in sport to stay. In 1972, Title IX, a national law, outlawed sex discrimination in academic and activity programs offered by educational institutions that receive funds from the government.   This omnibus education law opened the doors of sport, business and other professions to American women who had previously been severely limited in their access to all but the care-taking professions. American women were pressured to conform to a sex role stereotype that permitted them to be sex objects, decorative objects and caretakers (mothers, social workers, nurses, teachers and librarians).

Once they were allowed access to sport, the liberating effect of using one's strength and skills to achieve in a competitive environment had widespread impact. As a result, over the last 28 years, the stereotype of the ideal American woman has not only evolved to embrace physical activity and sport but other professions as well, from law and medicine to business and engineering. Women are being hired to perform in high pressure business and professional roles and their participation in sport is considered excellent preparation for such careers.

The increase in number of female sport participants has resulted in increases in the numbers of women in sport-related careers. However, it should be noted that this trend has followed participation entry at a very slow pace. Sharing the opportunity to participate is one thing; sharing access to sport profits and control of the sport economy is an entirely different matter.

The doors to employment in all sports related careers have only been open for several decades. But these doors have not opened very wide. In the USA, arguably the most liberal environment for women in sport-related careers, 80% of all coaches in school and college sport are still male. These numbers may be even more male dominated in youth sport, open amateur and professional sport. In general, the higher the status of the position and pay, the lower the proportion of female occupants. Thus, women continue to be almost non-existent in the most powerful decision-making positions in sport. If women are to make a really significant impact on the conduct of sport and the nature of this cultural institution, this barrier must fall.

New Economic Markets

Under the threat of loss of government funding, females in the USA had to be provided with equal opportunities to play and equal treatment and benefits in physical education, intramural, club and varsity sport programs. As a result, the number of girls playing varsity high school sports (ages 15-18) went from one in 27 to one in three (for boys, participation is one in two). Participation of girls in high school sports grew from 7% to 40% of all female students. At the college level (ages 18-22), participation of women grew from 16% to 40% of all athletes. Girls' and women's sports budgets expanded dramatically. Well-trained coaches and financial assistance exceeding $180 million per year is now being provided to female college athletes.

With regard to youth level sport (younger than 12 years old) girls in great numbers were exposed to organized soccer, baseball and basketball leagues via parent-led organized sport teams. The result over time has been that fifty-five million women now regularly participate in sports or fitness in the United States. Thirty-one million girls play team sports. Women represent 55% of all volleyball players, 43% of all runners and 41% of all soccer players. Economically, these sport participation opportunities have created three new, unique, large and potentially lucrative sports marketplaces: (1) the active female market, (2) the female as a spectator of men's sports and (3) male and female spectators of women's sports.

Active Female Market

Even though the physically active female consumer in the USA is less than 40 years old because Title IX has only been in force for 28 years, she has entered the critical consumer demographic of "18-34 female", the most desired and prolific consumer in America. As a result, U.S. corporations are rapidly repositioning to exploit and develop this market, one which has the potential of doubling the existing sporting goods industry. While the U.S. female was once a relatively narrow consumer of goods that enhanced her image as sex object, decorative object or caretaker (i.e., fashion, cosmetics, lingerie, household products, etc.) and purchased sports apparel and equipment for other members of her family, she is now buying such product for herself.

The respect of the female consumer is so important that numerous non-sporting goods manufacturers have already changed their advertising from portraying women in stereotypical ways to depictions of women as skilled athletes in order to be sure that customers know they recognize the many roles and choices of women. Because television is so widespread in America and important to the establishment of credibility and public opinion, this embrace of women's sport imagery has significantly influenced the public's perception of the skills and abilities of women in sport and its acceptance of her participation.

This active female consumer has also demonstrated that she is more eclectic in her sports participation than her male counterpart, making her an even more lucrative customer. American males are pressured from a very early age to participate in one of three or four of the most popular men's professional sports. Females are under no such constraints. Therefore, American girls and women have been in a better position to explore the worlds of dance, sport and exercise, and are now more likely to participate in a greater variety of such activities than males. Each of these activities requires different shoes, apparel and equipment, thus enhancing the economic value of female sport participants.

Females as Spectators and Consumers of Men's Sport
An unanticipated consequence of Title IX and the American gender equity sport movement has been an increase in numbers of female sports fans consuming men's professional sports products and licensed merchandise. When women were given the opportunity to play sports, they became as knowledgeable and as passionate about sports as their male counterparts. The female spectator currently comprises 35%-45% of the in-arena and television viewing audience of men's professional sports in the USA today. Every major men's professional league in ice hockey, baseball, football and basketball, has a sport-marketing staff specifically dedicated to develop the female market.

Males and Females as Spectators of Women's Sport
Another unanticipated consequence of Title IX was the explosion of female interest in team sports as participants and the interest of male and female spectators in women's sports. Prior to Title IX, women were restricted to more graceful, non-contact individual sports. There are now 18 women's

professional sports leagues in 13 sports, including six team sport leagues, in the USA. Television ratings are improving and corporate sponsorship of women's sports has more than tripled in the last decade. It is obvious that the development of women's professional sports will not take as long as the development of men's professional sports. The National Basketball Association, the dominant U.S. men's professional basketball league took 29 seasons to average 10,000 fans a game. The Women's National Basketball Association (WNBA) did it in two. Not only is there a large enough pool of elite female athletes to support professional sports leagues, there is an eager, loyal and interested spectator pool of males and females to support them.

The spectator pool for American women's sports is a separate market than the spectator pool for men's sports, both roughly 50% male and 50% female. This means an expanding sports spectator market that attracts investors and sponsors to women's professional sports leagues.

There is no reason to believe that the development of a global women's sports marketplace will not follow the American experience. Many national economies are moving toward capitalism and any market as large as the female sports market must be exploited. As women experience more economic success, they will participate in more leisure activities.

It is also important to note that even in non-capitalism based economies, higher socio-economic class women have always been permitted to pursue elite level participation. In addition, female athletes in socialist societies have, historically, been used to advance the perception of dominance of this particular political ideology. Indeed, most nations translate success on the playing fields of international sport into national pride, and the promotion and visibility of such successes have no gender boundaries. The publicly visible success of the female athlete produces generations of girls who aspire to follow in their footsteps. These aspirants become participants who consume athletic product and produce significant economic benefits. Such positive economic value will continue to be a significant impact of women entering sport.

Women's Impact on Sport Values

The impact of women on sport may be most considerable in the area of values. As children, boys and girls share similar values: fun, skill development, social interaction, and fair competition. In adulthood, men become preoccupied with the result of the competition while women value the process as well as the end product. Men's sports are more likely to embrace violence reflecting the historical roots of sport as preparing men for war. In the U.S.A., men's professional sport has also embraced poor sportsmanship, disrespect for opponents, and, on the professional level, a selfish pursuit of wealth and an arrogant disregard for rules of conduct and laws which govern the general public.

There are many who suggest that it is likely that women will begin to adopt men's sports values as women begin to receive the same opportunities to play and are coached by men and women who have embraced these values. However, one must also consider the possibility that men's sports will be positively affected and irrevocably changed as a result of the admittance of female athletes and their value system. The female athlete is bringing her own values to the playing fields and a likely result will be value changes on both sides. Many observers agree that it is unlikely that the female athlete will embrace sport violence because she is affected by the general societal issue of violence against women.

Value differences in the way women play sports are already clear in the rules of women's games. For instance, women's lacrosse is a non-contact sport while men's lacrosse is very contact-oriented. Women's ice hockey prohibits checking. Men's and women's basketball have the same rules, but are played very differently; men's basketball accepts a level of physical contact and checking that is not embraced by the women's game. Men's basketball audience values height, strength, contact under the boards, and muscling dunks over finesse shots. Women's basketball values teamwork, more passing, less contact, and more accurate shooting.

There also appears to be value differences in how male and female athletes relate to their fans. The female athlete, appreciating her new opportunities to play, appears to be extremely committed to community outreach and participation in promotional efforts. Male athletes respond more like sellers in a seller's market, more likely to view fans as an obligation or opportunity to charge for autographs or make profit from their role as celebrities. Professional male athletes increasingly appear to appeal to their high-priced corporate audiences while female professional athletes attract family audiences with affordable prices.

Audiences are also responding to male and female athletes in a different way which lends credence to male and female sport being different and a diversification of the appeal of the sports market. The women's sports fan appears to more closely identify with the female athlete sport experience compared to the fan of men's sports who is more an admirer of the superhuman specimen or the extraordinary.

While some would argue that is it only a matter of time before the female athlete takes on the value system of the dominant men's sports model, there are many who believe that the more likely outcome is that both men's and women's sport will change in response to the adaptation required to assimilate women's values. The values of female athletes and the nature of their games have caused men and women to question whether violence enhances or diminishes the sport experience. Is a free skating, fast and skill-oriented ice hockey game preferable to checking and physically preventing skilled execution of the elements of the game? Does hitting an opponent with a crosse enhance or detract from the game of lacrosse? Does a physical clash for positioning and rebounding under the boards, make basketball more or less interesting? At the very least, recognizing these differences and discussing them creates an environment where different is no longer considered "less than".

Thus, the impact of women in sport appears to permit greater variety and latitude in the way we play our games and our concept of what makes a skilled athlete. Much in the way that Sugar Ray Leonard cannot be said to be a lesser athlete than Mike Tyson, the female athlete is taking her place as different but talented player. Moreover, her values are being recognized as valid alternatives to the narrower scope of existing men's sport values.

Remaining Challenges

Women's impact on sport is being slowed by several other related realities: (1) the marginalization of female athletes and women's sports in the mass media, (2) the absence of all but a few professional women's sports leagues and (3) under representation of women in all sports related careers and especially in the decision-making hierarchy.

When the achievements of female athletes are not celebrated in the media in a highly visible and consistent way, as is true about the achievements of male athletes, the public's perception is that female athletes are not achieving. Thus, the culture's continued devaluing of women in sport is reinforced. There are several keys to adequate media coverage. When sport journalists are the products of a culture that has taught them to devalue women's sports participation, as is true with older sports journalists and decision-making editors and heads of sports programming, they are less likely to cover this aspect of sport. Female journalists and younger male journalists who grew up playing with female athletes and respecting their abilities simply are not the decision-makers. This situation will change over time.

Professional sports coverage dominates the sport media. If corporate advertisers and private investors do not invest in the professional women's sports product, reporting of men's professional sport will continue to dominate. One of the realities holding back the development of women's professional sports is the glut of men's sports products in the marketplace and the absence of prime time distribution outlets for the women's product. Most corporate dollars are in media advertising budgets. If women's sports are not televised, they do not access these considerable assets and are less likely to flourish. As the convergence of the Internet and television occur with virtually unlimited broadband transmission and reception, the ground for increased exposure of women's sports and corporate investment may become more fertile. It is in this environment that women's impact on sport will be both considerable and irreversible.

Summary

In summary, the sheer presence of large numbers of women as sport participants has ignited the powerful forces of change in the cultural institution of sport. Women's impact on sport has included the creation of three economic markets: the female as active sport participant, females as spectators of men's sport and males and females as spectators of women's sport. Women bring different values to sport and their sport competitions represent new sport product, different in kind than men's sport product. These differences in values will have an impact on men's and women's sports with women's sports moving more toward traditional men's sport values and men's sports being similarly impacted by women's values. However, until women's sport is embraced by the mass media and females occupy positions of decision-making power, change will be slow in this formerly all-male cultural institution that remains resistant to the inclusion of women and the sharing of power.

References and Bibliography

Acosta, R.V. & Carpenter, L.J. (1998). Women in intercollegiate sport: A longitudinal study-twenty-one year update, 1977-1997. Unpublished manuscript, Brooklyn College.

Bender, D. & Leone, B. (Eds.). (1995). *Male/Female Roles: Opposing Viewpoints*. Opposing Viewpoints Series. San Diego, CA: Greenhaven Press.

Berry, R.C. & Wong, G.M. (1986). *Law and business of the sports industries: (Volume II) Common issues in amateur and professional sports*. Dover, Mass.: Auburn House

Cahn, S.K. (1994). *Coming on Strong: Gender and Sexuality in Twentieth-Century Women's Sport*. New York: The Free Press.

Cohen, G.L. (1993). *Women in Sport: Issues and Controversies*. Newbury Park, CA: Sage Publications.

Creedon, P.J. (Ed.). (1994). *Women, Media & Sport*. California: Sage Publications.

Fausto-Sterling, A. (1992). *Myths of Gender: Biological Theories About Women and Men, 2nd ed*. New York: Basic Books.

Hargreaves, J. (1995). "A Historical Look at the Changing Symbolic Meanings of the Female Body in Western Sport." In van der Merwe, F. (Ed.). *Sport as Symbol, Symbols in Sport*. ISHPES Studies, vol. 4. Germany: Academia Verlag, 249-259.

Isaac, T.A. (1987). Sports - the final frontier: Sex discrimination in sports leadership. *Women Lawyers Journal, 73(4)*, 15-19.

Physical activity & sport in the lives of girls. (1997). Washington, DC: President's Council on Physical Fitness and Sports.

Wong, G.M. & Ensor, R.J. (1985-86). Sex discrimination in athletics: A review of two decades of accomplishments and defeats. *Gonzaga Law Review, 21(2)*, 345-393.

LEGAL ISSUES

The Role of Athletes and Agents

Annie Clement & *Paul Pedersen*

Introduction

Employment representation is a custom that has existed for years. It has become a common practice for business and industry chief executives to secure the services of a professional to negotiate their initial work agreements and examine major changes in their employment relationships. The reason most often given for creating a representation relationship is that the employee does not want to jeopardize his or her effective working relationship and "good will" with the employer by being forced to argue details of the working agreement. An ideal arrangement is one that permits the representatives of both the employer and employee to "hammer out" the technicalities of an agreement while the actual employer and employee discuss, with excitement and optimism, their future work.

A more recent phenomenon in employment representation is the headhunter. The task of this representative of management is to search for the best individual to fill a particular position within the company or organization. Often, the headhunter retains resumés for persons who are potential candidates for these positions. At other times, however, a headhunter may represent both employees and employers and work to bring the two parties together. Thus, the employment climate in the world today is such that those persons who seek top-level positions most often obtain help from professional representatives in valuing their skills and in locating jobs.

Correspondence to: Dr. Annie Clement, Esquire, Associate Professor, 110 Tully Gym, The Florida State University, Tallahassee, Florida 32306-4280, USA. E-mail: clement@mail.coe.fsu.edu

In addition to the headhunter in the corporate world, a representative of a writer or an actor is most frequently referred to as an agent. This individual works closely with the writer or actor in defining and expressing the person's skills, in preparing portfolios that are presented to publishers and production companies, and in locating employment and promotional opportunities. Here, the non-bias evaluation of skill plays a central role in the representation. The writers and actors look to their agents for such tough assessments. Agents also need to be as accurate as possible in making the assessments so that they will not become bogged down with unemployable weak talent and disgruntled clients. Furthermore, publishers and production companies are eager to build relationships and accept candidates when agents are adept at making good matches.

It is not uncommon to discover that neither the representatives of the employees nor the representatives of the employers have a specific title. More often than not, however, these employment professionals will be lawyers. This is especially true in the world of professional sport. As reported by Lipscomb and Titlebaum (2000), "over fifty percent of those actively involved as representatives at the present time in the four major professional leagues [United States] are lawyers" (p. 4). Most of those without a law degree still have significant knowledge of the law. The representatives, whether or not they are lawyers, are paid a percentage of the athletes' first year, renegotiated, renewed, or new salaries by the people they are representing or by the company that hired them. This fee is usually between three and five percent of the negotiated contract. In addition to contract negotiations, the functions of sport employment representatives can range from that of a simple friend to that of an all-purpose manager (Ruxin, 1993).

Beginning in the early 1970s, however, sport, particularly in the United States, became big business as the number of professional teams and athletic participants increased and the owner profits and player salaries soared. These changes resulted in tension between players and management that prompted athletes to consider representation. Similar to the quests of the chief executives, actors, and writers mentioned above, the players discovered that they needed expert non-biased assessments of their worth as athletes and opportunities to negotiate employment agreements for maximum value without facing the petty interpersonal problems that had many times lingered long after complicated negotiations. Thus, these athletes began to seek out representatives, called them agents, and asked for their help. They wanted the very same representation that top level business and industry executives, writers, and actors were afforded.

While most of the agents who have now helped to negotiate thousands of contracts are employment representatives with integrity, a few have slightly tarnished the image of agents. They have been able to do this by taking advantage of the system that is in place in professional and intercollegiate sports. Sport managers have historically used professional *scouts* to locate talent. Today, these scouts seem to play a more significant role in sport employment decisions than do similar scouts in executive, writer, and actor searches. Coaches of professional athletes, busy with a myriad of duties other than scouting, play a role similar to that of the managers in business and industry, publishing, and production. Therefore, the control that is given to scouts in professional sport means that sport managers accept the agents, not for their ability to value talent, but merely as negotiators of contracts. With this arrangement, the athlete seldom receives the agent's assessment of his or her talent and best fit for a particular organization. This treatment of agents by professional sport, coupled with the legislation of the National Collegiate Athletic Association (NCAA) which denies athletes the opportunity to be valued by an agent that will later obtain them employment, puts athletes at a disadvantage. It prohibits an athlete from receiving the single most important aspect of representation: a quality assessment of his or her skill and value by an unbiased professional. With the removal of the assessment of both the skill of an athlete and his or her value to a particular team from the representation formula, the doors have opened to a wide range of people who believe they possess the skills adequate to merely negotiate an athlete's contract. Furthermore, agents interested only in representing superstar players (those who will clearly attain the highest salaries), are now free from the difficult role of knowing how to assess physical skills and talent. As a result of this difference in the responsibilities of agents for sport and for other areas of employment, professional sport is faced with agents whose only skill is to obtain the best player and then to negotiate the best contract.

If all agents representing athletes had to possess the capacity to assess the skill of each athlete and assess the value of each athlete for a particular team, most of the agents considered a problem today would be quickly eliminated from the field. It should be noted that many highly successful sport agents and management companies value talent and are no different than the persons representing executives, writers, and actors. These sport agents fulfil the role of employment representatives by being capable of assessing talent and finding the best fit. It would appear that if the professional teams and the NCAA would give representatives the same role as that found in other areas of employment (i.e., assessing talent and best fit), the energy expended in controlling the actions of agents would be drastically reduced or no longer necessary.

The Structure of Professional Sport

Someone interested in representing athletes should become a student of the structure and governance of each sport in which he or she plans to work. Just as one would not enter into negotiations for a Hollywood actor without first becoming closely familiar with the movie industry, one should not consider employment representation of professional football players without first becoming thoroughly acquainted with the makeup of the National Football League (NFL). Furthermore, comprehensive knowledge of the history of the sport is a necessity. Considerable information can be gleaned from such sources as player association collective bargaining agreements, league constitutions and bylaws, and a number of articles and texts mentioned in this chapter and listed in its reference section.

In international law, a contract is fairly universal and contract law is similar from country to country. Employment law, however, is most often dictated more by local customs and accepted employment policies. While there are many ways to examine this topic, the most simplistic division in professional sport is by team and individual. The team sport structures presented in this chapter focus on football, men's and women's basketball, baseball, ice hockey and soccer. The individual sport structures addressed are women's and men's professional golf and women's and men's professional tennis.

Included in the discussion of each team and individual sport is the employment status of the athletes involved. Athletes in professional sport are either regular employees or independent contractors. In most cases, team sport personnel are regular employees or members of a specific team while individual sport professionals are independent contractors. A regular employee works for either the team owner, the person in charge of the company, or someone in the owner's chain of command. The owner controls the employee and is responsible or liable for the employee's actions. Under a regular employment relationship, the owner or individual in charge covers the employee's wages, unemployment insurance, worker's compensation, employment benefits, and other negotiated services. The European market provides services similar to the workers compensation and employee benefits found in the United States. Insurance is likewise influenced by the local government's role in health care. As opposed to a regular employee model, in an independent contractor relationship the employer has a contract right only to the task or project. For example, the task or project in golf or tennis would be the player participating in a specific tournament. The independent contractor pays a wage in a lump sum and does not cover unemployment insurance, worker's compensation, or benefits. Also, the employer is not liable for the torts of the employee. Theoretically, while a team owner could be held liable for the tort of a player, a person harmed by a tennis star during a match would find it difficult, if not impossible, to hold the owner of the tournament liable for the player's tort. For more information on employment law see Clement (1998) and Miller (1997).

American Football

There are a few professional football leagues in operation today. A couple of the more popular ones are the World Football League (WFL), Arena Football League (AFL), and the new XFL. This chapter, however, will focus on the National Football League (NFL). This league was inaugurated in 1920, in Canton, Ohio, USA. A rival league, the American Football League (AFL), was organized in 1960. Ten years later, however, the two leagues joined forces and began play as one league (NFL). Today, the NFL consists of two conferences and 31 teams. The champions of both conferences face each other in the Super Bowl. The 15 teams that comprise the National Football Conference (NFC) are separated into three divisions (east, central, and west). The teams in the NFC range from the storied franchises of the New York Giants, Dallas Cowboys, and Chicago Bears all the way to the newest addition, the Carolina Panthers. The American Football Conference (AFC) consists of 16 teams also separated into three similar divisions. Some of the more popular and successful teams in the AFC are the Denver Broncos, Miami Dolphins, and Pittsburgh Steelers. Home territory for a club is the city that holds the franchise and a 75-mile (120 km) radius from the city.

Since 1994, in an effort to ensure a level playing field, or equity in competition that translates into exciting, closely contested matches, NFL player salaries have been negotiated under a salary cap. This salary cap, which was a major part of 1993 Collective Bargaining Agreement between the NFL owners and the National Football League Players Association (NFLPA), was extended in 1998 through to the 2004 season. The salary cap is the maximum an organization is allowed to spend each year on player salaries. The dollar value of the salary cap (i.e., $62 million for 2000) is based on a highly sophisticated accounting system contained in the NFLPA Collective Bargaining Agreement. Additional information on salary caps can be found in the writings of Messeloff (2000). The average player salary for the 1999 season in the NFL was $1 million.

The players in the NFL are not independent contractors. Rather, they are considered regular employees. There are several labels under which the players are classified: rookies, i.e. players with less than three years of experience, restricted free agents, regular players, transition players, and franchise players. A thorough knowledge of each classification is essential for those interested in representing professional football players. Contract negotiations for young and inexperienced players (i.e., rookies and players with less than three years of experience) are less flexible than for experienced professionals. The football veterans are either regular (under contract) players or free agents. Free agents are either restricted or unrestricted. Restricted free agents are players with three completed seasons and an expired contract. Unrestricted free agents are players with four or more completed seasons and an expired contract. Within the free agent categories are also the transition (a club has first-refusal rights to match an offer given to a player by another club) and franchise designations. With the one franchise player a team is allowed each year, the club may match any other club's offer for its player, or receive two first-round draft choices if it decides not to match. The current collective bargaining agreement in the NFL was adopted in 1993 and expires in 2003.

Men's Basketball in North America

The National Basketball Association (NBA), which began play in November of 1946, has 29 teams comprising the Eastern and Western Conferences. The winners of each conference play in a best-of-seven series for the NBA Championship. The most legendary of the 15 franchises that make up the Atlantic and Central Divisions of the Eastern Conference are the Boston Celtics, New York Knicks, and Chicago Bulls. The 14 clubs of the Western Conference are divided into the Midwest and Pacific Divisions. Some of the more popular clubs from this conference are the Los Angeles Lakers, Houston Rockets, and Utah Jazz. Similar to the NFL, a 75-mile territorial right exists for each NBA club except where special privileges have been made (i.e., Los Angeles and New York/New Jersey).

The NBA has a salary cap and a specific system for defining basketball related income (BRI) and core basketball revenue (CBR). Unlike the NFL, however, the NBA has a specific salary cap (i.e., the preset figure for the 1999-2000 season was $34 million). While the bookkeeping systems used to determine the salary cap in the NBA is different from that which is used in the NFL, both are equally complex. An initial step in understanding the salary cap is to become familiar with the NBA Collective Bargaining Agreement which is detailed in the first volume of the work by Ganz, Gilmore, and Ressler (2000).

While a contract for an NBA player can be for any period of time, it cannot exceed six years. Contracts between veteran free agents and their prior teams may be up to seven years. A rookie contract may last for three years with one additional year. A number one draft pick may draw a salary as high as US$2.68 million for the first year and as low as US$535,600 for the last player selected in the first round. The average player salary for the 1998-99 season in the NBA was US$2.8 million. According to Ganz et al. (2000), the minimum salary for the 2000-01 season is US$316,969. In addition to the negotiated salary, the career-ending injury or illness clause is an important aspect. This part of the contract requires that a physician, selected jointly by the NBA and the NBA Players Association, makes the decision on what constitutes a career-ending injury or major illness. Also, the NBA Players Association has audit rights to review the books and records of the NBA League Office with reference to the BRI reports used in creating the salary cap.

Women's Basketball in North America

In June 1997, the Women's National Basketball Association (WNBA) held its first contest between the New York Liberty and the Los Angeles Sparks. Since its inaugural year of eight teams, the WNBA has expanded to 16 franchises that are separated into Eastern and Western Conferences. While the Houston Comets are the most successful team with three consecutive championships, the Indiana Fever, Miami Sol, Portland Fire, and Seattle Storm were added in the league's fourth year and are the newest teams. In the 2000 season, there were 176 players who played for the 16 teams.

The WNBA Players Association contract runs from 1999 through 2002. The players in this league are classified as regular employees. Their contracts, which on the average pay salaries of US$50,000, include both medical and dental insurance. Individual players in the WNBA sign one-year contracts with an option for renewal.

Baseball in North America

Despite a major strike in the mid-1990s that dampened interest in baseball, the sport known as America's favorite pastime has recovered and looks as strong as ever. While baseball is played by thousands of athletes from little leaguers to the minor leaguers, the pinnacle of success in North America is Major League Baseball (MLB). There are two leagues (American and National) with three divisions each (East, Central, and West) that makeup the major leagues. The American League (AL) consists of 14 clubs ranging from the new (Tampa Bay Devil Rays) to the legendary (New York Yankees, Detroit Tigers, and Boston Red Sox). There are 16 franchises that comprise the National League (NL). Among the more popular National League clubs are the Chicago Cubs, Cincinnati Reds, Atlanta Braves, and Los Angeles Dodgers.

New teams are added and existing franchises are allowed to move to a new city if they can obtain three-fourths of the membership vote. Exclusive territorial rights are the city in which each team resides and a ten-mile radius around the metropolitan area. After a gambling scandal almost destroyed Major League Baseball (MLB) in 1919, the AL and NL agreed to the use of one Commissioner. They have maintained that organizational structure since 1921. The Executive Council is composed of the Commissioner, the two league presidents, and eight other club members (four from each league).

Although MLB does not release individual player salary figures or payroll information for its 30 franchises, such data can be secured through secondary media sources. While most other professional leagues enforce a salary cap on their teams, there is no such restriction in MLB. With the arrival of free agency and salary arbitration, salaries of professional baseball players have skyrocketed from an average of $19,000 per season in 1967 to an average of $1.7 million for the 1999 season. Free agency, which the Major League Baseball Players Association (MLBPA) secured in the 1970s, allows players with six years of experience and without a contract to sign with any other team. Furthermore, players with 2.7 years of experience have the ability to have their salaries arbitrated. Since the first collective bargaining agreement between MLB and the MLBPA in 1968, minimum baseball salaries have risen from $10,000 to $200,000. Sixty-eight of the league's 830 players on opening day rosters in 1999 were making the minimum. The average salary for the 2000 baseball season was just over $2 million.

Ice Hockey in North America

The National Hockey League (NHL), which originated with five Canadian teams in November 1917, is presently a 30-member organization with 24 clubs in the United States and the remaining six franchises based in Canada. The NHL is separated into two conferences. The Eastern Conference, which has five teams in each of its three divisions (Atlantic, Northeast, and Southeast), consists of such storied franchises as the Boston Bruins, Montreal Canadians, New York Rangers, and Toronto Maple Leafs. Among the 15 clubs in the three divisions (Central, Northwest, and Pacific) of the Western Conference are the Detroit Red Wings, Edmonton Oilers, and Chicago Blackhawks. The NHL's two newest franchises, which began play in the 2000-01 season, are the Columbus Blue Jackets and the Minnesota Wild.

A National Hockey League Board of Governors oversees the NHL. The members of this Board manage the affairs of the League, establish policy, and select the Commissioner. Although the NHL began in Canada, its principal offices are now in New York City. The League conducts two annual meetings a year. The most recent collective bargaining agreement negotiated by the League and the National Hockey League Players Association (NHLPA) came about in 1995, and runs through to September of 2004. The NHLPA, in existence since 1967, bargains for nearly 700 professional hockey players. The average player salary for the 1998-99 season in the NHL was US$1.17 million. The Players Association, which is based in Toronto, certifies athletic agents and provides a training session for the agents each year. One of the two major concerns for the NHL is that, as a truly international business with teams in Canada and the United States, there is a need for constant attention to the financial dynamics in each country. The stabilization of resources among the large and small market franchises continues to pose a challenge to league leadership.

Soccer (Football)

Throughout recorded history, civilizations have played some form of soccer (known in many parts of the world as football). Although this is true for the Chinese, Greeks, Romans, Persians, Egyptians, and American Indians, the way soccer is recognized and played today took shape in England during the middle of the nineteenth century. The first attempt to standardize the game and establish rules was done in 1863, with the formation of The Football Assocation (FA). Throughout the 1870s there was a dramatic increase in football (soccer) clubs that accompanied the steep rise in the number of participants and spectators. In 1873, the Scottish Football Association was formed with its distinct style of play, in comparison with the English game. The English, however, introduced the world to professionalism in soccer in 1885 and to the first full-time league three years later.

Although soccer made its Olympic debut at the 1990 Games, it was not until the 1920s that the United States had a strong soccer league. But the American Soccer League was only a regional (Northeast) league. Thirty years later, the United States had two national soccer leagues after the formation of the United Soccer Association and the National Professional Soccer League. These two leagues merged in 1968 and became known as the North American Soccer League (NASL). Although there was a tremendous rise in the growth of soccer as a youth participant sport during the 1970s, the NASL struggled at the end of the decade and went bankrupt in 1984. The league, which had no television contract, had no problem raiding players from other countries but couldn't secure a national following and lacked a minor-league or college development system.

While outdoor professional soccer in the United States suffered for several years after the collapse of the NASL, the publicity surrounding the World Cups of the 1990s increased soccer enthusiam and resulted in the formation in 1996 of Major League Soccer (MLS). This relatively new league has grown with its strong corporate sponsorship setup, television contracts, and attendance. With teams consisting of American players and a limited number of international stars, MLS is structured as a single-entity league which means that all teams are owned by the League. In this sports structure, which is unique in the United States but more common throughout the world, all of the teams and player contracts are owned by the League rather than individual franchise owners. MLS and other similar international sports leagues use this structure to eliminate the financial disparities between large and small markets, control player costs, offer commercial affiliates an integrated sponsorship and licensing program, and allow for decisions to be made that are in the best interest of the entire League rather than just one team. Teams in MLS, as in the case with other professional sports leagues, are permitted to trade players with League approval.

Women's Golf

The Ladies Professional Golf Association (LPGA) is a nonprofit corporation that was founded in 1950. This Association, which is the longest-running, independent professional sports organization for women, sponsors 43 tournaments each year, four of which are Majors (Nabisco Championship, McDonald's LPGA Championship, U.S. Women's Open, and du Maurier Classic). Under the leadership of LPGA Commissioner Ty Votaw, the total purse for all the LPGA Tour events during the 2000 seasons was in excess of US$36.2 million, a Tour record.

LPGA Tour golfers are independent contractors and arrange to play a select number of tournaments each year. Therefore, these professional golfers do not earn a fixed salary. Rather, they base their income on their performance at individual events in which they choose to participate. Some of the more popular participants are Nancy Lopez, Beth Daniel, Se Ri Pak, Karrie Webb, and Annika Sorenstam. The discrepancy between LPGA Tour player earnings is quite dramatic, as they range from US$500 a year to over US$1.5 million.

Men's Golf

Founded in 1916, the Professional Golfers Association (PGA) of America began in New York with 82 charter members. This association, in addition to conducting numerous programs to promote the game of golf, ran 47 tournaments in 2000 for PGA Tour players. The major tournaments on the PGA Tour are The Masters, the U.S. Open, the British Open, and the PGA Championship. Similar to the LPGA Tour golfers, the participants in the PGA Tour are independent contractors who do not earn a fixed salary from the PGA. Although legendary golfers such as Jack Nicklaus, Arnold Palmer and Gary Player can mostly be seen on the Senior PGA Tour, the PGA Tour is loaded with another group of international superstars led by Tiger Woods, David Duval, and Ernie Els. Woods is in a class by himself as he made US$15 million playing golf in 1999. However, his endorsements that year raised his total salary to around US$50 million. Overall, purses in the PGA Tour have risen from US$69 million in 1995, to nearly US$150 million for the 2000 season.

Agents work with both female and male professional golfers to solicit sponsorships and develop promotional packages. The typical sponsorship for the golfer who has yet to earn a Tour Card provides that the contractor will pay the expenses of the athlete in exchange for a percentage of the future winnings and endorsements contracts. Once the golfer gets a Tour Card, the representative works closely with the professional athlete to secure endorsement contracts. The negotiating fees for endorsements can be as much as 25% of the contract value.

Women's and Men's Tennis

Tennis, originally called lawn tennis, can be traced to a 12th century French handball game. Early tennis organizations were the U.S. National Lawn Tennis Association (formed in 1881), the British Lawn Tennis Association (1888), the Lawn Tennis Association of Australia (1904), and the French Federation of Lawn Tennis (1920). In 1975, the national governing body for tennis in the United States was renamed the U.S. Tennis Association (USTA). Today, the International Tennis Federation (ITF), the world governing body for tennis, sanctions the rules by which organized tennis is played.

During its early years, professional tennis consisted of barnstorming tours featuring reigning champions and amateur challengers. In 1967, the National Tennis League and World Championship Tennis (WCT) began competition to sign the best professional and amateur players. Open professionalism had arrived by 1968, and with it, major championships and eventual tens of millions of dollars in prize money. Soon thereafter, professional athletes formed separate men's and women's player unions known as the Association of Tennis Professional (ATP) and the Women's Tennis Association (WTA). In 1986, the WTA changed its name to the Women's International Tennis Association (WITA).

Professional tennis circuits, which consist of major tournaments such as Wimbledon and the U.S. Open, have been governed by the Men's and Women's International Professional Tennis councils since the late 1970s. These groups work with the ATP Tour and the WITA Tour. ATP Tour players have ranged from Jimmy Connors and Björn Borg to Pete Sampras and Andre Agassi. WITA Tour professional athletes are former players such as Martina Navratilova, Chris Evert, and Steffi Graf and current players such as Martina Hingis and Venus and Serena Williams.

The 150-plus members in each of the two professional tennis guilds are independent contractors. Therefore, similar to golf, tennis is an individual sport in which the income potential for star athletes is virtually unlimited with opportunities for very lucrative player earnings and endorsements.

The Professional Athlete

For decades, the baseball club that first signed a player to a contract owned the athlete for the rest of the athlete's professional career. The "reserve clause," which was first written into the standard player's contract in 1887, prohibited an athlete for his entire career from negotiating with another club. However, the franchise that owned the player could release or trade the athlete at any time for any reason. For example, Babe Ruth, the legendary baseball player, was initially the sole property of the Boston Red Sox. Ruth, in addition to not having a say in his eventual trade to the New York Yankees, was bound by the reserve clause to stay with the Yankees even if he wanted to play for another club.

It was not until the arrival of free agency and the elimination of the reserve clause in 1975, that a veteran athlete could move to another club if his contract had expired. The NHL, which had a similar reserve clause to that of MLB, eliminated its reserve clause in 1972, in favor of the system used by the NBA and NFL. The NBA and NFL have always used the less restrictive option clause, which binds a professional basketball or football player to his team for just one year after the expiration of a contract.

Sport as a Product

Professional team sports have always had a rather unique approach to labor standards. Sport, because its product is competition rather than the game itself, is different to other businesses. For example, in the automobile industry, the product is the car, not the speed at which a particular assembly line can produce a car or the difference between a striped down or a luxury model. According to Clement (1998), "For sport competition to be successful in the entertainment market, play must be exciting and lively with a close score throughout the event. The exciting, lively, close score encounter is most assured when a 'level playing field' has been established prior to competition. To create a 'level playing field' or equal skills, players must be allocated to competing teams on the basis of skill and talent so all teams in a league have an equal start. Drafts, trades, salary caps, etc. are among the systems used to create this equality" (p. 197).

Labor Law in the USA

United States labor law evolved from Article One of the Constitution and was systematically developed through the Sherman Act of 1890, Clayton Act of 1914, Norris-LaGuardia Act of 1932, National Labor Relations Act, a result of amendments to the Wagner Act of 1935, and the Taft Hartley Act of 1948. These acts worked to grant numerous rights to employees and unions.

Major League Baseball was the first sport to resort to the courts and labor law to gain professional athletes a working relationship similar to that found in business and industry. In the case of *Federal Baseball Club of Baltimore v. National League of Baseball Clubs* (1922), a complaint brought against the "reserve clause," the plaintiffs attempted to use the "interstate commerce clause" of the Sherman Act as their legal support. Supreme Court Justice Oliver Wendell Holmes ruled for professional baseball saying that baseball was a state or local event and not controlled by interstate commerce. In 1953, a second attempt to change the work agreement by arguing that the baseball player reserve system violated antitrust law also failed (Toolson v. New York Yankees, 1953). In 1972, baseball player Curt Flood, after being traded to another team without his knowledge, brought a cause of action against the Commissioner of Baseball for antitrust violations. The Supreme Court noted that baseball had operated successfully since 1922, under the antitrust exemption and therefore should not be changed, except through a challenge by Congress.

After the 1972 Flood decision, Players Associations became important to all team sports and began to negotiate contract after contract slowly removing many of the severe controlling factors. However, a careful analysis of the player agreements of contemporary athletes will find contract requirements far more management friendly than would be found in the computer or entertainment industries. Sport is an industry where, for most employees, the greatest talent will be expended in the early years of employment. An athlete's tenure may be as short as three years and as long as ten. Skill value usually resides with youth. Because of this unique short career time span, it is a necessity for athletes to be free to move from team to team without restraint and to make as much money as possible while they retain their youth.

Although contemporary bargaining agreements appear to be player friendly to the public, upon closer inspection most would find these sport industry agreements quite restrictive. Clement (1998) and Yasser, McCurdy, and Goplerud (1997) provide comprehensive discussions of labor law as it relates to professional sports.

Team Sports Bargaining Agreements

Because the Players Associations in team sports can be considered league associations, all player bargaining agreements are the same as union agreements in other industries. A Player Association (i.e., MLBPA, NFLPA, etc.,) negotiates a detailed contract for a specific period of time (usually between four to ten years) with the management of the league. Team owners participate in setting the agreement details and all owners must abide by the agreement. Basic components of the contract are player services, compensation (i.e., salary, bonuses, and incentives), termination, appearance, licensing, representation, drugs, on-the-field and off-the-field conduct, hazardous activities, skill and training, and the resolution of disputes. Often a minimum salary will also be agreed upon and posted within the agreement.

Employment arrangements in the United States are at-will, contract, or union bargaining agreements. The team sports professional is under a union bargaining agreement. Unlike other business agreements, team sports professionals must accept the bargaining agreement and then, if sufficiently talented, negotiate a contract addendum for additional benefits. In business and industry the employee either joins a union and accepts the bargaining agreement or negotiates an individual contract. Team sports athletes take both arrangements.

Researchers suggest that many workers have neither the benefit of a contract or a collective bargaining agreement. Such individuals are considered at-will employees. At-will means that an employer and employee agree to work together for the mutual benefit of both parties. If one of the parties wishes to terminate the agreement, notice of desire to terminate is given to the other party, along with the length of time before termination. While a reasonable notification of termination is between a week to a couple of months, the most popular time period is a two week notice. The highly skilled athlete sees the at-will work arrangement as the one that would most satisfy his or her interests.

Individual Sports Agreements

Because of the wide variety of sports, numerous types of contracts are encountered by individual sports participants. As mentioned earlier, commonality among individual sports is not high. Within some sports, players may join a tour and the tour contract will contain many of the elements mentioned above. In other sports, however, a separate contract will be negotiated for each event or competition. While the terms, money, skill, and performance expectations will be similar, the handling of appearance, licensing, and representation may be difficult. The agent or athlete representative needs to be aware of tournament and tour constitutions, bylaws, guidelines, and contracts. Further, financial security of the event and the agency running the event must be investigated. Contract terms for cancellation (i.e., because of the weather) and medical emergencies are key contract components that need to be agreed upon.

Regulation of Agents by Athletic Associations and State Agencies

Until the 1970s, player contracts were most often negotiated by the athletes themselves. This phenomenon changed with the proliferation of agents over the past 30 years (Ruxin, 1993). While the majority of player representatives are ethical individuals, a few have been corrupt. As a result of the scandals that have surfaced regarding some of these unscrupulous agents, effort has been made by the sports leagues, athletic associations, and state governments to certify and to some extent, control the actions and conduct of player representatives.

In addition to regulation by state agencies, the National Collegiate Athletic Association (NCAA) is explicit in its advice on eligibility. An amateur athlete can obtain information on his or her skill value and contract viability, but may not use the same person for his or her agent when eligible to obtain representation. As a result, agents often ignore and then violate NCAA rules sacrificing a player's collegiate eligibility. Some overly enthusiastic and unethical agents, competing for contracts, go as far as to shower athletes (i.e., prospective clients) with gifts in an effort to obtain their employment.

California was the first state to pass agent legislation in 1981. The majority of the states now have some form of agent legislation. State legislation allows for civil and criminal sanctions for those agents who fail to follow the rules. In addition to protecting the athletes themselves, the regulations by state agencies are also directed toward protecting the universities and colleges from receiving harsh sanctions that could be handed down due to the work of just one unscrupulous agent.

Regulation of Representatives by Players Associations

The National Basketball Players Association (NBPA) creates a list of certified agents. A player who chooses not to represent himself must use an NBPA-approved certified agent to negotiate his contract. For agents to be certified, they must have a college degree from an accredited college or university; fill out a detailed form containing information on qualifications, special training, experience, past representation; pay a fee; provide the league office a statement of each individual player's compensation agreement; and permit an audit of the agent's firm. Furthermore, certified agents are also required to report any violations of NBPA rules by their player to the league office. Compensation to the agent for a minimum contract is $2,000 and 4% of all monies in excess of the minimum contract. In the event that a dispute arises between any of the parties, the NBPA requires that the NBPA's selected arbitrator be used.

The Major League Baseball Players Association (MLBPA) also certifies player agents. However, a person who has completed the MLBPA agent certification requirements is not certified until he or she represents an athlete with the Association.

The National Hockey League Players Association (NHLPA) requires that a player either represents himself or uses a certified agent to negotiate all NHLPA contracts. In applying for certification the agent must detail his or her relevant education, training, experience in negotiations, past representation, and business associations or memberships. The agent, in addition to attending an NHLPA seminar, must know the NHL structure, applicable bargaining agreements, and developments in sport law and related subjects.

Similar to the other Players Associations, the National Football League Players Association (NFLPA) also certifies agents to negotiate with their affiliate clubs. Requirements are basically the same as those listed above with the MLBPA, NBPA, and NHLPA. The one major exception, however, is that the negotiation fee for the player representative must be 3% or less of the contract. Any person contemplating representation of an athlete must obtain all necessary materials, attend the required orientation seminars, and provide full application prior to initiating an agreement.

Agencies Representing Athletes

Today, many agents are affiliated with large sport management firms. These companies provide comprehensive support for athletes ranging from endorsement negotiations to tax advice and from investment counseling to personal services. Examples of such management firms include the International Management Group (IMG), SFX Entertainment, Advantage International, and Proserv.

The Future

Futurists tell us that in this new millennium industry will see an intense focus on the valuing of employees. This valuing of skilled workers, if accepted by the sport industry, will result in even larger compensation packages than exist today for athletes. It will be the agent who will negotiate these new opportunities.

Should the countries of the world choose to copy the American sport industry as the British have done in their use of a management company from the United States to plan Wimbledon, opportunities for professional athletes will grow exponentially as will their support staff, including representatives. In contrast, a backlash by sport spectators who can no longer afford to view live game play could result in all countries of the world returning to the local and Olympic model of sport with inexpensive spectator seats for a vast array of events available to the masses.

References

Clayton Act, 15 U.S.C. 4 and 6 (1914).

Clement, A. (1998). *Law in sport and physical activity*. Tallahassee, FL: Sport and Law Press.

Federal Baseball Club of Baltimore v. National League of Baseball Clubs, 259 U. S. 200 (1992).

Flood v. Kuhn, 316 F. Supp. 271 (1970) and 443 F. 2d 264 (1971) and 407 U.S. 258 (1972).

Ganz, H.L., Gilmore, K. R., & Ressler, J. (2000). *Business and legal aspects of the sports industry*. (Volumes I & II). New York, NY: Practicing Law Institute.

Lipscomb, C.B. & Titlebaum, P. (2000). Selecting a sports agent: Finding the perfect fit. *For the record*, 11(3), 2-4.

Messeloff, D. (2000). The NBA's deal with the devil: The antitrust implications of the 1999 NBA-NBPA Collective Bargaining Agreement. 10

Fordham I.P. (1997) *Media and Entertainment Law Journal*, 521.

Miller, L.K. (1997). *Sport business management*. Gaithersburg, MD: Aspen.

Norris LaGuardia Act, 29 U.S.C. 102 (1932).

National Labor Relations Act, 29 U.S.C. 127.

Sherman Act, 15 U.S.C. 1 and 2 (1890).

Toolson v. New York Yankees, 346 U. S. 356 (1953).

Yasser, R., McCurdy, J.R., & Goplerud, C.P. (1997). *Sports law, cases and materials*. Cincinnati, OH: Anderson.

Bibliography for Non-Specialists

Clement, A. (1998). *Law in sport and physical activity*. Tallahassee, FL: Sport and Law Press.

Ruxin, R.H. (1993). *An athlete's guide to agents*. Boston: Jones and Bartlett.

Yasser, R., McCurdy, J.R., & Goplerud, C.P. (1997). *Sports Law, cases and materials*. Cincinnati, OH: Anderson.

Bibliography for Specialists

Closius, P.J. (1999). Hell hath no fury like a fan scorned: State regulations of sport agents. 30 *University of Toledo Law Review*, 511.

Couch, B. (2000). How agents competition and corruption affects sports and the athlete-agent relationship and what can be done to control it. *Seton Hall Journal of Sport Law*, 10, 111.

Cozzillio, M.J. & Levinstein, M.S. (1997). *Case Law*. Durham, NC: Carolina Academic Press.

Ganz, H.L., Gilmore, K.R., & Ressler, J. (2000). *Business and legal aspects of the sports industry*. (Volumes I & II). New York: Practicing Law Institute.

Messeloff, D. (2000). The NBA's deal with the devil: The antitrust implications of the 1999 NBA-NBPA Collective Bargaining Agreement. Fordham I.P., *Media & Entertainment Law Journal*, 10, 521.

Remis, R. & Sudia, D. (1999). Escaping athlete agent statutory regulation: Loopholes and constitutional defectiveness based on tri-parte classification of athletes. *Seton Hall Journal of Sport Law*, 9(1).

THE TEAM WITHIN THE TEAM IN PROFESSIONAL SPORT

National Football League (NFL) Model

Vernon Cheek

Introduction

The *National Football League* (NFL), one of the first professional sport leagues in the world, is presently one of the most prominent worldwide in professional sport. The *Super Bowl,* in existence for the past 35 years, is one of the most watched sporting events in the world via television and the Internet. What has brought the NFL to such prominence worldwide?

Part of the answer lies within the heroes of the sport: (1) the athletes; (2) the coaches; and (3) the behind-the-scenes support team. Athletes frequently headline the news, do the most interviews, and win the games that can get a team to the Super Bowl or World Championship. The athletes come from various backgrounds and a variety of football systems. This diversity is complex and results in great debate about the medialization of professional athletes. Coaches are responsible for motivating the athletes. Several of them make million dollar salaries; many do not. They are responsible for guiding the majority of millionaire athletes in positive directions. Coaches must know how to blend athletes into systems or systems with athletes. The behind-the-scenes support team members scout professional and collegiate athletes, evaluate performances of the athletes on their team as well as on the other 31 teams in the National Football League. Their job titles range from general manager to assistant coach, and their focus is bringing the best athletes and characters to a professional football team. The often unnoticed group of heroes involves the behind-the-

Correspondence to: Vernon Cheek, Publications Director, Seattle Seahawks, 11220 NE 53rd St. Kirkland, WA 98033, USA. E-mail: VernonC@Seahawks.com scenes support team, most importantly the *scout* and the *salary cap specialist*.

The Scout

As a scout, this member of the behind-the-scenes team evaluates athletes on an annual basis. Scouts evaluate athletes from a number of sources, including the other 31 teams in the NFL, all collegiate football programs and even semi-professional leagues. There are athletes in the NFL whose contracts expire at the end of each year. Each team may want to bring these athletes into their system. There are collegiate athletes at all levels who warrant an opportunity to try out for the team. There are also athletes in semi-professional leagues who have excelled who are offered opportunities to try out. Numerous collegiate post-season awards that reward athletes for outstanding play are factored into the equation, and, more importantly, make decision makers on professional teams more aware of talents. These factors contribute to tremendous competition for the best talent available.

It all begins, unofficially, in the month of May, when behind-the-scenes support team members sit down and review film from the previous season. What are they looking for? Did an athlete give up when the team was losing 45-0? When an athlete dropped a touchdown pass, did he display the determination needed to get open again and catch the next one? How did the quarterback perform? Has the factor of age contributed to which athletes play at key positions? How important is the first round draft choice this year to the future of the program? Did the first round draft choice perform up to expectations or is he a career reserve athlete? These are just some of the questions the scout must consider in the month of May.

To illustrate these points, St. Louis Rams quarterback, Kurt Warner, distinguished himself in 1999 when he led the Rams to the Super Bowl, setting records and proving his critics wrong along the way. Warner did not go immediately to the St. Louis franchise after playing collegiate football. He was a member of the *Arena Football League* and what is presently referred to as *NFL Europe*. While playing for the Amsterdam Admirals, he had the opportunity to refine his skills. Those skills attracted the scouts of the Rams who presented him with the opportunity to join this professional team.

NFL Europe has become a melting pot for athletes who seek to improve their skills and have a place in the training camp of a NFL team. Athletes who have used this route to gain a place in the NFL include La'Roi Glover from Barcelona to the *New Orleans Saints,* Jay Fiedler from Amsterdam to the *Miami Dolphins*, and Marcus Robinson from the *Rhein Fire* to the *Chicago Bears.*

When the month of June approaches, the scout has already begun determining the primary candidates for the team's 80-man roster. Some areas may need more attention than others, but the following information provides a framework for qualities of a professional quarterback.

Athlete Evaluation
When evaluating a quarterback for the NFL, critical and secondary factors are included. *Critical factors* include throwing accuracy, ball velocity, intelligence, quarterback height, and work ethic. The *secondary factors* include leadership, mobility, competitiveness, overall production, fundamental skills performance, experience, athletic ability, and stability.

Kurt Warner's accuracy in 1999 was record setting. He was repeatedly able to complete passes in critical situations for positive results. His peripheral vision on the field and his throwing finesse led the Rams to the Super Bowl. Warner also studied the habits of the opposing team's defensive secondary, was able to read certain defensive formations, particularly in critical situations, and anticipated when it was best to focus on one, two or even three receivers in offensive situations.

A scout would determine if Warner could successfully throw passes that lead receivers in routes such as a 16-yard comeback, 16-yard in, and a 20-yard post. All quarterbacks at the NFL level need to be able to throw these passes in a dynamic game-like environment.

A quarterback's intelligence is monitored continuously from youth to the last touchdown pass he throws in a major Bowl game before he enters the NFL. Does he make decisions quickly and accurately? Who coached him? What kind of reputation does that coach have? What were his intelligence scores on qualifying examinations used for college/university entrance? What type of grade point average did he earn while in college?   Are his fundamental skills appropriate for elite competition?

Figure 1 is an example of a typical checklist of critical and secondary factors used to determine a quarterback's readiness to play in the NFL:

Athlete: _____	Date: _____
Critical Factors	Mobility
Accuracy	In the Pocket
Completion %	Ability to scramble
Vision	Throw on the run
Touch	Footwork agility
Film, workout	Competitiveness
Consider drops	Toughness – Mental / Physical
Anticipation	Can he take over a game?
Ball Velocity	Performance under pressure
Intelligence	"Big play" ability
Grade point average; scores	Production
Football "Smart"	Other statistics: Touchdowns,
Interview	Interceptions, Quarterback rating
Ability to learn	Sacks, fumbles, etc.
Quick mind	Red Zone, 3rd down performance
Who was his coach?	Fundamentals
Film decisions	Release level
Height	Release quickness
6'2" minimum	Drops
Must play like a BIG man	Specific throwing mechanics
Exceptions must be special	General ball handling
Work Ethic	Experience
Practice	Level of competition
Extra physical prowess	Years / Games started in college
Extra mental effort	Potential / Improvement factor
Off-season	Athletic Ability
Measure desire	Box score
	Speed
Secondary Factors	Agility
Leadership	Workout
Personality, coachability	Stability
Others play better when he plays	Tap score
Trust	Past problems
	Interview
	Reliability

Figure 1. Quarterback Readiness: Critical and Secondary Factors

A grading system is also utilized throughout the entire National Football League for every athlete at every position. The system may vary from team to team (depending upon the general manager), but the system has proven effective in determining what type of athlete each team is in need of in order for the team to progress to the next level.

Most NFL teams' Grading Systems are divided into colors, ranging from Red to Green. A *Red athlete* is considered to be an impact athlete, while a *Green athlete* is one who will be replaced as soon as possible. Table 1 represents a typical NFL Team Grading System.

Minnesota Vikings wide receiver, Randy Moss, is considered to be a Red athlete throughout the League. He is an impact athlete and is of *Pro Bowl* quality. Some individuals would argue that not too many Red type athletes exist in the NFL.

Grade			Comment
RED			This is an impact athlete of *Pro Bowl* Quality.
	RED	1.0	
	RED	1.5	
	RED	1.8	
ORANGE			This is a productive, talented performer. Most teams will win with this athlete.
	ORANGE	2.0	He makes a difference to the team and game when playing.
	ORANGE	2.5	
	ORANGE	2.9	
BLUE			This is a solid NFL starter. He would upgrade most teams.
	BLUE	3.0	
	BLUE	3.5	
	BLUE	3.9	
PINK			Starter or Backup. Can play in the league, but ideally club would like to upgrade.
	PINK	5.0	
	PINK	5.5	
	PINK	5.9	
GREY			A young athlete of some promise and talent who has not yet had the production or playing time to determine exact level.
	GREY	6.0	
	GREY	6.5	
	GREY	7.0	
GREEN			An athlete needing to be replaced as soon as possible.
	GREEN	8.0	
	GREEN	8.5	
	GREEN	8.9	

Table 1: Typical NFL Team Grading System

Systems are also in place throughout the NFL for college athletes. The scout provides the athlete with a grade and then projects in what round the college athlete could be drafted. Figure 2 provides an example of this type of determination and prediction.

CATEGORY	AREA FOR THE FUTURE

Exceptional **Exceptional Player**
An exceptional player; he is the truly exceptional prospect; he will be a starter; he is a potential *All-Pro* and could be a candidate for 1st year awards by the League and various national outlets.

Super **Super Player**
A dominant athlete; a potential *All-Pro* and *Rookie-of-the-Year* candidate once the skills are developed. A certain starter provided there is no exceptional individual at the position.

High Average **High Average Starter**
A potential starter his first year. Will be, at worst, a strong backup his first year. Will become a starter in a limited amount of time.

Could Start **Could Start**
Will make the active roster and should contribute his first year at a position or as a situational athlete. Should develop into a starter in 2-3 years.

Difference Maker **Difference Maker**
Could be the difference between making the active roster and playing a vital role on special teams. He should make the roster. Should develop into strong backup in 2-3 years and could go on to become a starter if he realizes and reaches his potential. Strong prospect to back up. Must help on special teams.

Should Make It? **Should Make It?**
A prospect. He may eventually help your team. He has a better than an even chance to make it in the League.

League Wide Talent **League Wide Talent**
Have more than one redeeming quality that would encourage you have them as part of your team. Some will command larger salaries than others.

Might Make It? **Might Make it?**
Might make the team, but has to work hard and there's no promises.

College Material **College Material**
He is not eligible to be drafted. Will have an additional year of eligibility at the college level.

Need More Information **Need More Information**
Was unable to evaluate due to lack of complete data. That might include lack of video tape, dropped out of school, etc.

Will Not Make The Team **Will Not Make The Team**
Not a NFL prospect. Most teams state why he's not a NFL prospect.

Figure 2: Grading and Prediction Chart

The scout must also determine answers to the following questions: Who gets drafted? Who will become part of the future of the team? Will it be the first round draft choice who ranked highly in all of the grades listed above, or will it be the mid-level athlete who many teams reject?

At this point, the 80-man roster has been filled. The all-important *depth charts* are now put into place as the team begins the pre-season games in preparation for the regular season. The scout's "to do" list is now broken into daily and weekly lists. The daily lists include game film, sport scans, injury reports, preparing the athlete board, waiver wire activity, and individual athlete reports. The weekly lists include depth charts, advance scouting (reports), updating the emergency board, preparing for weekly workouts, updating the agent list, and preparing travel credentials (plans).

Updating the emergency board is particularly critical because the incidence of injuries is a reality, and the scout must know what athletes are unable to participate and must be replaced by healthy athletes. This same reason is used if an athlete is not playing up to potential.

The Salary Cap Specialist

The business of orchestrating a professional football team starts with the salary cap. In the 2000 season, teams had a limit of $67,000,000 US to spend on athlete salaries. This money was used to contract the eleven athletes on offense, defense, and special teams. A salary cap specialist also has to divide the money available to the all-important backup athletes. By the July training camp, there must be 80 separate salaries on record by the time the team takes the practice field.

A good analogy for a salary cap specialist is the credit card. When a purchase is made, a limit is provided to maximize spending. If the entire balance owed is not paid within a month, monthly payments must be made until the entire balance is paid. Teams can defer payments to athletes for years, but the deferments count against the salary cap and is, therefore, known as a cap number.

An example of the salary cap concept is provided by examining the salary of player John Elway, *Denver Broncos* quarterback:

- Elway was scheduled to make $4.2 million US in salary during 1997. For NFL accounting purposes, his team also had to count $1.1 million US from his previous signing bonus. Accordingly, Elway's total 1997 charge against the cap was $5.3 million US.
- Elway received $565,000 US in salary during 1997, a $2.26 million US signing bonus that was prorated over five years (at $452,000 US annually) for cap purposes, and a $1.1 million US roster bonus in March, 1998.
- The team counted $1.1 million US from Elway's previous signing bonus against the 1997 salary cap.
- Elway's new charge against the Broncos' 1997 cap figure was then slightly over $2.1 million US, thereby clearing $3.2 million US for Denver's 1997 cap total and deferred it into future cap years.

Once the NFL athletes' contract is due, or when a restructuring is in order, the salary cap specialist has the responsibility of making the athlete and his agent comfortable with the salary. When the salary cap is successfully renegotiated and the athlete makes more money under the cap, it is a viable but costly adjustment for the team. That new contract now means that the athlete will receive the same money, but it will be spread out over a longer period of time, similar to the credit card analogy.

Baltimore Ravens' Director of Administration, Pat Moriarty, understands the salary cap, but explained things in a different way:
"We had a pretty good season in 2000 and made the big plays when we had to by acquiring key athletes in the off-season like Pro Bowler defensive tackle, Sam Adams. Athletes of that caliber have to be paid at some point. The true heroes from a financial perspective are the athletes who are your starters and making league minimum. Those athletes are helping the organization win and, at the same time, we're winning the salary cap battle because we have more to spend on athletes down the line." (Personal communication, January 12, 2001)

There has to be a balance in financial commitment from the organization. The salary cap specialist strives to keep that balance. Some quarterbacks in the NFL illustrate this type of commitment. A second string quarterback, Scott Mitchell, who played behind the legendary *Miami Dolphins',* Dan Marino, made a big name when he took advantage of his playing time.

Marino was in his prime, and the Dolphins were forced to make a decision on Mitchell who received great reviews from scouts throughout the NFL. The logical decision would have been to keep both quarterbacks. The salary cap specialist, however, informed the team that if two high-priced quarterbacks are hired, another area of the team suffers and salaries would have to be paid for years to come.

The legendary athletes, Walter Payton and Jim Brown could never play on the same team in their prime in today's game. Both athletes were great running backs, and both would command huge salaries on today's open market.

Most teams attempt to find a good mix of veteran athletes who, serving as the nucleus of the team, will cost them substantive money in salaries, along with a few second tier athletes and draft choices who will have smaller salary contracts.

The salary cap specialist knows how much money the NFL team can spend on an athlete(s), and he knows how much it will cost the team for years to come. If salaries are broken down into percentages by position, 21% of a team's money will be spent on the offensive line. Many upper management individuals feel a good offensive line is the key to winning championships.

The defensive line is second, at 17%. The defensive line also contributes dramatically to a team's success. The *Baltimore Ravens* defensive line ranked Number One in the NFL in 2000, and set the record for fewest points allowed in a season. A large amount of the credit went to the defensive line that featured Michael McCrary, and 2001 Pro Bowler, Sam Adams. The Ravens made the decision to upgrade the defensive line by signing Adams to a large contract in the off-season.

Defensive backs rank third, at 13%. For many teams, the defensive secondary is the last line of defense to prevent a touchdown. Teams are willing to place substantial money into the position of defensive back. Wide receivers and linebackers tie for salary cap money, at 12%. The quarterback's percentage is, on an average, 12%. In the 21st century game, there must be a solid starter, an experienced backup, and a good third string quarterback. All teams have begun to realize that even with the best quarterback, an offensive line has to give him time to throw if the offense is to be effective.

Runningbacks are next at 7%. There are a lot of quality runningbacks in the NFL. Tight ends are next at 5%. A good tight end can catch a critical third down pass. Finally, the special teams athletes are listed at 2%.

The typical salary cap specialist will contemplate the following questions as the season progresses: How much money was spent on the offensive line? How much money is the quarterback making? Is there a three or four year athlete in the backfield who warrants a large contract? What are the receivers earning? Is one of them leading the league in catches after just his first or second year? Is there a potential star athlete on the defensive line who has been consistent in getting to the quarterback? What should be paid? Why?

In summary, those who are hired as members of the behind-the-scenes support team, particularly the scout and the salary cap specialist, play vital roles in the success of the team at the National Football League level. While little has been written about the two positions, the information shared in this chapter provides a unique insight into the underpinnings of a professional football franchise. As the business of sport becomes increasingly competitive, the role of the scout and the salary cap specialist will increase in importance. Both roles contribute to the dynamics of professional sport competition as the ultimate in sporting entertainment.

References

Walsh, B., Billick, B., Peterson, J. (1998). *Bill Walsh, Finding The Winning Edge*. Champaign, IL: Sports Publishing Inc.

NFL Management Council and The NFL Players Association, (February 25, 1998). NFL Collective Bargaining Agreement 1993-2005.

Seattle Seahawks Public Relations Department (1999). *Seattle Seahawks 1999 Media Guide*. Kirkland, WA

National Football League Member Clubs (2000). NFLMC Labor Seminar in Dallas. New York, NY

Personal Interviews

Glasgow, Nesby - Director of Player Programs, Seattle Seahawks: December 15, 2000

Reinfeldt, Mike - Senior Vice-President, Seattle Seahawks: January 6, 2001

Moriarty, Pat - Vice-President Administration, Baltimore Ravens: January 12, 2001

Wright, Gary - Vice-President Communications, Seattle Seahawks: November 11, 2000

Lewis, Will - Director of Pro Personnel, Seattle Seahawks: October 7, 2000

Wyllie, Tony - Vice-President Communications, Houston Texans: October 28, 2000

PERSPECTIVES VOLUME 3:
THE BUSINESS OF SPORT

Business and the Olympic Movement:
A Commentary

Matthias Kleinert
DaimlerChrysler AG

As an example of the growing significance of sport in today's society, the 2000 Olympic Games in Sydney were a resounding success, with 199 countries taking part and rave reviews from athletes and spectators alike. Clearly, the Olympic Games continue to fascinate the world.

It is easy to see why. Sports are one of the few activities in which people of every race, culture and creed can meet to compete in a non-aggressive setting and on equal footing. The Olympics, in particular, are not only a venue for athletic competition, but also a festival of humanity, friendship, solidarity and world peace. Only against this sporting backdrop was it possible for the two Koreas to unite briefly when their teams entered Sydney's Olympic Stadium together – an otherwise inconceivable event.

Today more than ever, the Olympic movement seeks to promote international understanding; to further dialog among civilisations, nations and individuals. This is why DaimlerChrysler is an active supporter of the Olympic Movement. Its partnership with the International Olympic Committee and other key organisations in international sport reflects the company's understanding of its responsibility toward society. The ideals of sport incorporate the same ideals that DaimlerChrysler leadership shares.

Correspondence to: Mr. Matthias Kleinert, Senior Vice President, International Relations and Corporate Business, DaimlerChrysler AG, D-70546 Stuttgart, Germany

Ideally, competition should take place under the aspect of fair play and sportsmanship. This means not only giving the best, but also accepting limitations and restrictions in giving that best; that there are referees who have the final say. The same holds true for DaimlerChrysler.

DaimlerChrysler is a global player, with some 450,000 employees worldwide. Its partnership with the IOC is especially dedicated to promoting sport in less developed countries. To this end, the IOC, its member organisations, and DaimlerChrysler run a wide variety of projects and programmes which, among other things, seek to make the leaders of underdeveloped countries a part of sport and the Olympic Movement. Given the nature and dimensions of the problems in many such nations, the IOC can offer only limited direct financial aid. For this reason, the IOC must turn to reliable partners for its developmental programmes.

As part of the "Olympic Solidarity" programme, DaimlerChrysler donates Mercedes-Benz vehicles and means of transportation to National Olympic Committees so that athletes can be transported to training sites and competitions. Here, priority is given to the National Olympic Committees in developing countries. The "Olympafrica" project, which concentrates on the Southern African region, enables funding for joint programmes that set up sport and training facilities for children and young people.

DaimlerChrysler also invests over one billion DM (deutsche mark) a year in environmental protection. As a company operating globally, DaimlerChrysler deals with the interaction of economics, ecology, technology, and "internationality" every day and endeavours to sustain an environment appropriate for sport and leisure pursuits. As such, the corporation leadership has a responsibility towards every society – not only to our shareholders, customers and employees, but all of the people with whom the corporation interacts.

Sport emphasises values such as perseverance, team spirit, self-discipline, fairness, tolerance and the desire to do one's best. These are values that DaimlerChrysler also embraces, for without them, the corporation could not continually be a top performer in international competition. That is why DaimlerChrysler's sponsoring activities also seek to advance the goals and values that business, society and sports share.

Responsibility towards society also includes promoting co-operation between culture and business. For this reason, DaimlerChrysler sponsors culture programmes and events, and works to further the cross-cultural aspects of the world through sport. In this way, sport, business and culture form a mutually beneficial, interactive triad, and it is to this end that DaimlerChrysler has become the main sponsor of the German Football Association. The Preamble of this agreement states that the co-operative efforts between DaimlerChrysler and the German Football Association will concentrate on social responsibility at home and abroad. Both partners, as stated in the agreement, will jointly initiate and promote activities and projects that enhance international understanding and solidarity. In particular, these undertakings will focus on children and young people.

Corporate philosophy and culture at DaimlerChrysler, therefore, work not only towards profitability, strengthening the company in the face of global competition, customer satisfaction, and good returns on shareholder investment. Supporting the ideals behind sport is just one means of attaining this goal.

INFORMATION SECTION

Resources and Contacts for the Business Professional

1. INTERNATIONAL ORGANISATIONS

ICSSPE – International Council of Sport Science and Physical Education

ICSSPE is an umbrella organisation with a diverse range of over 220 member organisations world-wide. The Council promotes and disseminates a wide range of scientific information, and has a co-ordinating function with national and international organisations, as well as a close relationship with UNESCO and the IOC. In addition to facilitating communication and exchange of information world-wide in all aspects related to sport science and physical education.   Effective management is an issue for all organisations and associations involved with sport.   ICSSPE promotes an atmosphere where multidisciplinary issues related to sport science have a forum for communication.

ICSSPE's comprehensive website is updated on a regular basis to share knowledge, report events, and announce newly published resources. It is just one of the tools ICSSPE uses to build stronger international cooperation and bridge the gap between developed and developing countries. There is also a link to the SIRC Calendar, for details about upcoming events.

ICSSPE/CIEPSS Executive Office	Tel:	+49 30 805 00360
Am Kleinen Wansee 6	Fax:	+49 30 805 6386
14109 Berlin	E-mail:	icsspe@icsspe.org
GERMANY	Internet:	www.icsspe.org

SMAANZ - Sport Management Association of Australia and New Zealand

The Sport Management Association of Australia and New Zealand is the regional association dedicated to enhancing and facilitating sport management research throughout the two countries comprising its membership. An annual conference is held (usually in November) which typically attracts academics and practitioners and the emphasis is on presenting the latest research emerging from within Australia and New Zealand. Increasingly, the conference is attracting international delegates from a variety of universities and countries. SMAANZ also produces the journal, *Sport Management Review*, currently published two times per year in May and November. *Sport Management Review* has published manuscripts from local academics as well as a number from international researchers.

Prof. David Shilbury, President Ms Linda Van Leeuwen, Secretary Sport Management Program Faculty of Business, UTS PO Box 222 Lindfield NSW 2070 AUSTRALIA	E-mail : linda.van.leeuwen@uts.edu.au Internet: www.gu.au/school/lst/servies/ smaanz/smaanz.htm

EASM - European Association for Sport Management

The European Association for Sport Management (EASM) is an independent association of individuals involved or interested in the management of sport in the broadest sense. The aims of EASM are to promote, stimulate and encourage studies, research, scholarly writing and professional development in the field of sport management.

The Bureau of the Association, based in Firenze (Italy), provides services and information to current and potential members, keeps and develops contacts with sport organisations and universities in Europe, and manages and develops relationships with international organisations.

The main activities of the association are:

• A Newsletter with the latest information on the activities of the Association and the general development in the field all over the world.

• The production of the *European Sport Management Quarterly*. The Journal covers a wide range of sport management topics, ensuring proper balance of practical application and theory.

• An annual Congress hosted each year in a different European country. Offering scientists and professionals an opportunity to discuss the basic issues and latest topics in the field.

Prof. Dr. Livin Bollaert, President EASM Bureau ISEF Firenze Viuzzo di Gattaia 9 50125 FIRENZE ITALIA	Fax : + 39 55 241799 E-mail : easm@cesit1.unifi.it Internet: http://www.easm.org

NASSM - North American Society of Sport Management

NASSM recognises an essential common body of knowledge in sport management that is cross-disciplinary and relates to management, leadership, and organisation in sport; behavioural dimensions in sport; ethics in sport management; sport marketing; communication in sport; sport finance; sport economics; sport business in the social context; legal aspects of sport; sport governance; and sport management professional preparation.

NASSM's official research journal is the *Journal of Sport Management*. The journal embraces research focusing on the theoretical and applied aspects of management related to sport, exercise, dance, and play. Journal research focuses on sport management in a variety of settings such as professional sport, intercollegiate and interscholastic sport, health/sport clubs, sport arenas, and community recreational sports.

Karen Danylchuk	Fax : +44 (519) 661-3937
School of Kinesiology	E-mail : karenduan@julian.uwo.ca
Thames Hall, Room 3170C	Internet: http://www.nassm.org
The University of Western Ontario	NASSM Listserve: <sportmgt@unb.ca>
London, ON N6A 3K7	

1.2 Regional Organisations

College Athletic Business Management Association

CABMA, the College Athletic Business Management Association, is an organisation devoted to the establishment, maintenance and implementation of the highest standards of integrity and efficiency in the scope, policies and procedures involved in the management and administration of business in the athletics departments and associations of colleges and universities.

In addition to serving the colleges and universities of the United States, Canada and Mexico, CABMA makes available associate memberships to companies and organisations in business and industry whose functions and activities are related to intercollegiate athletics. This type of membership not only benefits the associate member but enables the associate member to provide service, consultation and advice to the regular membership.

CABMA serves its membership, in the following manner:

- The organisation promotes individual contact and knowledge-sharing between members. Expertise in any area becomes accessible to all.

- An annual convention, featuring an outstanding program covering many timely subjects. The convention is currently held in conjunction with the NCAA convention in January.

- Active committees work year-round to improve the organisation, encourage membership, plan the annual convention and program, and assist institutions throughout the country in solving problems.

- Awards, including the coveted "Manager of the Year", are presented annually to members who have excelled in the execution of their duties and responsibilities in their institutions.

For information contact: Brian Horning CABMA Membership P.O. Box 16428 Cleveland, OH 44116 USA	Tel: + 440-892-4000 Fax: + 440-892-4007 Email: bhorning@nacda.com Internet: http://www.cabma.com

2. SPORTS MANAGEMENT DEGREE PROGRAMS

The following institutions have been located with Sport Management programs (ordered alphabetically)

Australia

Canberra University	www.science.canberra.edu.au/sportstud/
Deakin University	www.deakin.edu.au/bowater/sport_mgt/spmgt
Southern Cross University	www.sessm.scu.edu.au/sportmanagement
University of Technology Sydney	www.business.uts.edu.au/leisure/index
Ballarat University	www.ballarat.edu.au/academic/business
Edith Cowan University	www.cowan.edu.au/acserv/hb2001/ug/bpm/
Griffith University	www.gu.edu.au/ua/aa/hbk/fsbussub1.html

Canada

Brock University	www.brocku.ca/spma
University of British Columbia	www.educ.ubc.ca/hkin
Concordia University	www.commerce.concordia.ca/diasa.htm
Laurentian University	www.laurentian.ca/www/spad/index.htm
University of New Brunswick	www.unb.ca/kinesiology/sportmanagement.htm
University of Regina	www.uregina.ca/~pasweb/
Mount Royal College, Alberta	www.mtroyal.ab.ca/programs/commhealth/physed/
University of Western Ontario	www.uwo.ca/fhs/kinesiology/graduate.html
University of Alberta	www.per.ualbera.ca/

Europe

University of Groningen, Netherlands	www.waner-advies.nl/
De Montfort University, England	www.dmu.ac.uk/dept/schools/pesl/welcome
University of Barcelona	www.ub.es/eoe/esport.html

New Zealand

Massey University	www.massey.ac.nz/
University of Otago	www.divcom.otago.ac.nz

United States of America

Ball State University	www.bsu.edu/cast/pe/grad2.htm
Baylor University	www.baylor.edu/~hhpr/graduate/sportmanagement
Bowling Green State University	lindah@bgnet.bgsu.edu
Brooklyn College of New York	ctobey@brooklyn.cuny.edu
Canisius College	www.canisius.edu/canhp/departments/spadm
Central Michigan University	www.cmich.edu/gradpes
Clemson University	www.clemson.edu/market/sarsport
East Tennessee State University	www.etsu.edu/gradstud/index.htm
Florida State University	www.fsu.edu/~phys-ed
Georgia Southern University	www2.gasou.edu/RASM/RASM.HTM
Georgia State University	www.gsu.edu
Grambling State University	www.gram.edu
Indiana State University	grdstudy@amber.indstate.edu
Lynn University	admission@lynn.edu
Millersville University	gradstu@marauder.millersv.edu
Mississippi State University	www.msstate.edu/dept/pe/pe.html
Ohio University	www.ohiou.edu/~sportadmin
Old Dominion University	www.odu.edu/~esper/graduate.html
Radford University	gdarden@runet.edu
Rutgers University	www.exsci.rutgers.edu
Seton Hall University	mayoann@shu.edu
Slippery Rock University	graduate.studies@sru.edu
Southern Illinois University	clox@siue.edu
State University of New York	gradadmit@brockport.edu
St. Thomas University	www.stu.edu/promang/sports/new_spo_home.htm
Temple University	www.temple.edu/STHM
United States Sports Academy	www.sport.ussa.edu/program1.htm
University of Alabama	www.uab.edu
University of Connecticut	playlab.unconn.edu/dept.html
University of Georgia	www.gradsch.uga.edu/
University of Florida	www.aa.ufl.edu/fellows/index.html
University of Illinois	cary-m@uiuc.edu
University of Kentucky	www.uky.edu/education/khp/smhead.html
University of Massachusetts	www.umass.edu/sptmgt
University of Miami (FL)	www.education.miami.edu/department/ess/ess
University of New Mexico	www.unm.edu/~sportad/

United States of America continued...

University of North Carolina	www.unc.edu/depts/exercise/sa_cover.html
University of Northern Colorado	www.unco.edu/sptadm
University of Oklahoma	www.ou.edu/cas/hss/smangrad.htm
University of South Carolina	www.aps.sc.edu/spta/sportad.html
University of Tennessee	www.coe.utk.edu/spa
University of Wisconsin	www.uwax.edu/graduate/index
Wayne State University	www.hpt.wayne.edu
Westchester University	www.wcupa.edu/users/mipe/grad/sptmgt
Western Illinois University	www.wiu.edu/users/mipe/grad/sptmgt
Xavier University	www.xu.edu/admissions/graduate/sportadm

3. PUBLICATIONS

Please note: An extensive two-tier bibliography is located at the end of each chapter and includes a wide range of journals and monographs relating sport management and administration. Resources listed at the end of each chapter are relevant to both specialists and non-specialists. Below is a list of selected journals and internet sites. Please refer to each chapter for monographs and additional specific resources.

3.1 Journals

♦ **Journal of Sport Management**. Journal of the North American Society for Sport Management.
  < http://www.unb.ca/web/SportManagement/nassm.htm >

♦ **Australian journal of management.** Journal of the Australian Graduate School of Management, UNSW.
  < http://www.agsm.unsw.edu.au/~eajm/>

♦ **International Journal of Sports Management.** Published by American Press. Boston, MA.

♦ **Journal of Sport and Social Issues.** Official journal of the Center for the Study of Sport in Society, Northeastern University.
  < http://www.northeastern.edu/>

- **Marketing Science.** Published by The Institute of Management Sciences and the Operations Research Society of America
- **Sport Management Review.** Journal of the Sport Management Association of Australia and New Zealand
  www.gu.au/school/lst/servies/smaanz/smaanz.htm>
- **Sport Marketing Quarterly.** Published by Morgantown, WV: Fitness Information Technology.
- **Journal of sport history.** Produced by the North American Society for Sports History < http://www.nassh.org>

3.2 Reference Books/Book Series

The following publications represent a selection of book series which complement the extensive list of publications already identified by the author of each chapter.

- American Sport Education Program (1996). *Event management for sport directors.* Champaign, IL.: Human Kinetics.
- Bucher, C. & Krotee, M. (1998). *Management of physical education and sport.* Boston: WCB/McGraw-Hill.
- Byl, J. (1999). *Organizing Successful Tournaments 2nd ed.* Champaign, IL: Human Kinetics.
- Cameron, J. (1996). *Trail blazers: Women who Manage New Zealand Sport.* Christchurch, N.Z.: Sports Inclined.
- Chelladurai, M. & Packianathan, J. (1999). *Human Resource Management in Sport and Recreation.* Champaign, IL: Human Kinetics
- Daily, J. (2000). *Recreation and Sport Planning and Design.* Adelaide: Recreation Sport and Racing.
- DeSensi, J., Rosenberg, D. (1996). *Ethics in Sport Management.* Morgantown, WV: Fitness Information Technology.

- Flannery, T. (1999*). Personnel Management for Sport Directors.* Champaign, IL: Human Kinetics.

- Howard, D. & Crompton, J. (1995). *Financing sport.* Morgantown, WV: Fitness Information Technology.

- Leith, L. (1990). *Coaches Guide to Sport Administration.* Champaign: Leisure Press.

- Martens, R. (1995). *Youth Sport Director Guide.* Champaign, IL: Human Kinetics.

- Mull, R. et al. (1997). *Recreational sport management 3rd ed.* Champaign, IL: Human Kinetics.

- McKay, J. (1991). *No Pain, No Gain. Sport and Australian Culture.* Sydney: Prentice Hall.

- Mullin, T. (2000). *Sport Marketing, 2nd ed.* Champaign, IL: Human Kinetics.

- National Association for Sport and Physical Education/North American Society for Sport Management. (1993). *Sport management program standards and review protocol.* Reston, VA: Author.

- National Association for Sport and Physical Education/North American Society for Sport Management. (1999). *Sport management program review registry.* Reston, VA: Author.

- *Soucie, D. (1998). Research in Sport Management – ICSSPE Sport Science Studies vol.9. Schorndorf: Verlag Karl Hoffmann.*

- Parks, J. Zanger, B. & Quarterman, J. (Eds). *Contemporary sport management.* Champaign, IL: Human Kinetics

- Shilbury, D., Quick, S. & Westerbeek, H. (1998). *Strategic Sport Marketing.* Sydney: Allen & Unwin.

- Shilbury, D. & Deane, J. (1998). *Sport management in Australia: an organisational overview.* Burwood, Vic.: Bowater School of Management and Marketing, Deakin University.

- Smith, A. & Stewart, B. (1999). *Sports Management. A Guide to Professional Practice*. Sydney: Allen & Unwin.

- Trenberth, L. & Collins, C. (1999). *Sport Business Management in New Zealand*. Palmerston North, New Zealand: The Dunmore Press.

- Stier, W. (1994). *Fundraising for Sport and Recreation*. Champaign, IL: Human Kinetics.

- Stier, W. (1997*). More Fantastic Fundraisers for Sport and Recreation*. Champaign, IL : Human Kinetics.

- Vamplew, W., Moore, K., O'Hara, J. Cashman, R. & Jobling, I. (Eds.) (1992). *The Oxford Companion to Australian Sport*. Oxford University Press: Melbourne.

- Vanderzwaag, H. (1998). *Policy Development in Sport Management*. Westport, Conn: Praeger.

In addition, there are many important and high quality book series which have been published to introduce, promote, develop and enhance specific managerial and administrative activities globally and more specifically with relation to sports.

3.3 Congress/Workshop Proceedings

Proceedings of the European Congress of Sport Management from 1994 to 1999, will soon be available on CD-ROM. For more information, please contact EASM.

Shilbury, D. & Chalip, L. (Eds.) (1997*). Advancing Management of Australian and New Zealand Sport. Conference Proceedings*, 2nd Annual Sport Management Association of Australia and New Zealand Conference. Southern Cross University, November 1996.

Australia New Zealand Sports Law Association (1997). *200 Towards 2000*. Proceedings of the 7th Annual ANZSLA Conference, Newcastle.

4. INTERNET RESOURCES

4.1 Data Banks

Although there is not yet a specific sports management database, sports management research and journals are listed in numerous search indexes. Popular indexes are listed below:

- *Leisure, Recreation and Tourism Abstracts*,
- *Sport Search*,
- *Sport Database*,
- *Physical Education Index*,
- *Faxon Finder*
- *Sports Documentation Monthly Bulletin*,
- *SPORTDiscus*,
- *Focus on: Sports Science & Medicine*, and
- *Research Alert*

Information data banks can also be located at:

Sport Information Resource Center for information/collections addressing sports, fitness and related fields:
<http://www.sirc.ca/>

University of Connecticut Laboratory for Leisure, Tourism & Sport for free reference lists in numerous sport-related areas:
<http://playlab.uconn.edu/frl.htm>

4.2 Additional Internet Resources

Athens Organising Committee for the Summer Olympic Games
<http://www.athens.olympic.org/gr/>

> Athens will be the host for the next Summer Olympic Games in 2004. The Athens 2004 site contains information on the volunteer programme, objectives and information from the Organising Committee, including progress reports, updates from the `newsroom' on the latest Olympic news and opportunities for employment.

Australian Sports Commission <http://www.ausport.gov.au/home.html>

This site contains a variety of information including: sport organisation in Australia, competition calendars and details, contacts for International sport, information on sports, athlete profiles, issues and topics in sport, jobs available, publications, AIS facilities and training information and images.

Business resource center <http://www.morebusiness.com/>

More business is a site on general business, including articles, newsletters and tools for finding further information. A great site for finding business specific information. Updated weekly.

Business Europe <http://www.businesseurope.com/>

From daily business news to 'how-to' guides, this site includes indepth, regularly updated information on: Finance, sales and marketing, e-commerce, technology, office and people, travel and transport.

Hillary Commission, NZ <http://www.hillarysport.org.nz/>

The Hillary Commission for Sport Fitness and Leisure has been set up by the Government to develop sport and physical activity so that more people can be involved, enjoy an active lifestyle and develop their skills - perhaps even become champions. The Commission's main role is to fund sport and active leisure organisations and sports clubs in New Zealand.

International Olympic Committee <http://www.olympic.org>

The website for the IOC contains news and information from the IOC, its National Olympic Committees and links to the following sites: Organising Committees for coming Summer and Winter Olympic games, the Olympic Museum, the Olympic Collectors site, Olympic Television Archive Bureau, the World Anti-Doping agency and the International Sports Federations.

Salt Lake City Organising Committee for the Winter Olympic Games
<http://www.saltlake2002.com/>

Official site of the 2002 Winter Games in Salt Lake City. The site includes the latest information from the Organising Committee, calendars of events, Olympic news and information on athletes and events.

Sporting Goods Business <http://www.sportstrend.com>

This site contains news and information on the sporting retailers, public relations, the state of the market, sporting goods dealers and trade shows.

Sport Management Information Center
<http://www.unb.ca/web/SportManagement/>

The site contains links to the three major International Sport Management Organisations: EASM, NASSM and SMAANZ and contains details on Conferences, University programs, links to various sport management related sites and suggested internet search tools for related information.

The Sports business daily   <http://www.sportsbizdaily.com>

The *Sports Business Daily* is the first daily trade publication dedicated to the business of sports. *Sports Business Daily* delivers news to its clients every business day. Clients receive essential sports industry news while it is still fresh, helping them to make more informed business decisions. The site covers: sponsorship, endorsements, labor relations, licensing, team ownership, marketing, advertising, broadcasting and public policy.

Torino Organising Committee for the 2006 Winter Games
<http://www.torino2006.it/ita/index.html>

Official site of the 2006 Winter Games in Torino. The site includes information on the progress of games organisation and Olympic news and information on athletes and events.

5. Computer Products

Sport Director: Professional Edition 1.0
Sport Director: Volunteer Edition 1.0
The above products can be ordered from Human Kinetics (www.hkusa.com)

This resource information section was compiled with assistance from Darlene A. Kluka, Ph. D., Charles T. Smith Jr., B.S., Terry Lilly, M.S. and David Ponton, M.S from the Department of HPER, graduate students enrolled in SPA 525, Fall, 2000, Grambling State University of Louisiana, USA.